T0328656

Cambridge Elements ≡

Elements in the Philosophy of Law
edited by
George Pavlakos
University of Glasgow
Gerald J. Postema
University of North Carolina at Chapel Hill
Kenneth M. Ehrenberg
University of Surrey

LEGAL PERSONHOOD

Visa A. J. Kurki
University of Helsinki

CAMBRIDGE
UNIVERSITY PRESS

CAMBRIDGE
UNIVERSITY PRESS

Shaftesbury Road, Cambridge CB2 8EA, United Kingdom

One Liberty Plaza, 20th Floor, New York, NY 10006, USA

477 Williamstown Road, Port Melbourne, VIC 3207, Australia

314–321, 3rd Floor, Plot 3, Splendor Forum, Jasola District Centre,
New Delhi – 110025, India

103 Penang Road, #05–06/07, Visioncrest Commercial, Singapore 238467

Cambridge University Press is part of Cambridge University Press & Assessment,
a department of the University of Cambridge.

We share the University's mission to contribute to society through the pursuit of
education, learning and research at the highest international levels of excellence.

www.cambridge.org
Information on this title: www.cambridge.org/9781009462235

DOI: 10.1017/9781009025614

First published 2023

A catalogue record for this publication is available from the British Library

ISBN 978-1-009-46223-5 Hardback
ISBN 978-1-009-01647-6 Paperback
ISSN 2631-5815 (online)
ISSN 2631-5807 (print)

Cambridge University Press & Assessment has no responsibility for the persistence
or accuracy of URLs for external or third-party internet websites referred to in this
publication and does not guarantee that any content on such websites is, or will
remain, accurate or appropriate.

Legal Personhood

Elements in the Philosophy of Law

DOI: 10.1017/9781009025614
First published online: November 2023

Visa A.J. Kurki
University of Helsinki
Author for correspondence: Visa Kurki, visa.kurki@helsinki.fi

Abstract: This Element presents the notion of legal personhood, which is a foundational concept of Western law. It explores the theoretical and philosophical foundations of legal personhood, such as how legal personhood is defined and whether legal personhood is connected to personhood as a general notion. It also scrutinises particular categories of legal personhood. It first focuses on two classical categories: natural persons (human beings) and artificial persons (corporations). The discussions of natural persons also cover the developing legal status of children and individuals with disabilities. The Element also presents three emerging categories of legal personhood: animals, nature and natural objects, and AI systems. This title is also available as Open Access on Cambridge Core.

This Element also has a video abstract: www.Cambridge.org/Kurki_abstract

Keywords: legal person, corporation, legal personhood, legal personality, person

ISBNs: 9781009462235 (HB), 9781009016476 (PB), 9781009025614 (OC)
ISSNs: 2631-5815 (online), 2631-5807 (print)

Contents

Introduction

Legal personhood, or legal personality, is a foundational concept of Western law. Legal persons are most often understood as those beings that hold rights and/or duties, or at least have the capacity to hold rights, under some legal system. That born human beings are legal persons is a keystone of modern human rights law – the right to "recognition everywhere as a person before the law" is mentioned in the Universal Declaration of Human Rights. However, historically, some human beings have been denied full legal personhood. The most central examples include slaves and women.

Slaves are often considered a paradigmatic example of treating human beings as property and nonpersons, even though many scholars agree that the situation was not as black-and-white as it is occasionally depicted.[1] Women have also historically been denied at least some aspects of legal personhood in many Western jurisdictions, even though the status of women has varied from jurisdiction to jurisdiction. A classic example is the common-law doctrine of coverture, under which married women's legal status was, in many regards, subsumed into that of their husbands. Joanne Bailey describes this as "the legal fiction that a husband and wife were one person".[2]

In legal theory and philosophy, the notion of legal personhood was for decades a relatively peripheral topic. However, in the recent years, various developments have made legal personhood contested and debated once again.

On one hand, some "classical" subjects relating to legal personhood have become increasingly topical, or at least retained their relevance. First, the legal status of foetuses remains highly controversial, primarily because of its connection to the question of abortion rights. US discussions of foetal personhood have become increasingly relevant after the overturning of *Roe* v. *Wade* in June 2022.[3] As the right to abortion is no longer entailed by the US Constitution, states now

---

[1] In ancient Rome, slaves could for instance own property with their master's permission, and in the antebellum US, slaves were in some regards treated as legal persons under criminal law: they could be prosecuted and could appeal their convictions. See e.g. Richard Gamauf, "Slaves Doing Business: The Role of Roman Law in the Economy of a Roman Household" (2009) 16 European Review of History: Revue europeenne d'histoire 331; Andrew Fede, *People without Rights: An Interpretation of the Fundamentals of the Law of Slavery in the U.S. South* (Garland 1992); Alan Watson, *Roman Slave Law* (The Johns Hopkins University Press 1988); Thomas D Morris, *Southern Slavery and the Law, 1619–1860* (The University of North Carolina Press 1996).

[2] Joanne Bailey, "Favoured or Oppressed? Married Women, Property and 'Coverture' in England, 1660–1800" (2002) 17 Continuity and Change 351. However, as with slaves, there are shades of grey to be found. For instance, Bailey notes that under coverture, "[a] husband gained outright permanent possession of all his wife's moveable goods and had the right to manage his wife's land and to receive its rents and profits during marriage, though he required his wife's sanction to dispose of it". ibid 352. Hence, given that the wife's sanction was required, the husband and the wife were not strictly speaking "one person" in all regards.

[3] *Dobbs* v. *Jackson Women's Health Organization*, No. 19-1392, 597 U.S. (2022)

enjoy significantly more freedom in determining the legal status of foetuses and embryos.[4]

Another classical subject is the corporation, or so-called *artificial* or *juristic person*. The idea of corporations as goes back to Roman law and is shared by all Western legal systems. Scholars debated theories of corporations vigorously from the nineteenth century onwards, but by the latter half of the twentieth century, the debate had mostly died down. The great legal philosopher HLA Hart stated in his inaugural address in 1953 that "[i]t is said by many that the juristic controversy over the nature of corporate personality is dead".[5] However, philosophers and legal scholars have begun to show an increasing interest in the nature of corporations. Issues of a more political nature remain relevant as well. Modern business corporations, in particular, are often subject to questions such as whether the owners of business corporations can exploit the limited liability structure of the corporation to avoid responsibility.[6] The status of corporations is particularly fraught in the US because of the idiosyncratic US doctrine according to which corporations are also constitutional persons, meaning that they enjoy some constitutional rights.

On the other hand, emerging categories of legal personhood have upset traditional boundaries of legal personhood. Scholars, activists and policymakers debate the legal personhood of animals, ecosystems, and AI systems. Advocates of animal legal personhood have achieved some relatively limited victories, whereas the Rights of Nature movement – demanding that nature or some parts of nature be given rights or legal personhood – has been quite successful in some parts of the world.[7] Even though AI legal personhood is still mostly a theoretical idea at the time of writing of this Element, the startling development of AI may turn it into reality quickly.

This Element is intended to make sense of these developments and debates. The first two sections of the Element will discuss legal personhood on a general level. Section 1 scrutinises what is meant by legal personhood and compares different accounts of the notion. Section 2 delves deeper into a number of philosophical and theoretical issues underlying legal personhood, such as the question of whether legal personhood must be connected

---

[4] Carliss N Chatman, "If a Fetus Is a Person, It Should Get Child Support, Due Process, and Citizenship".

[5] HLA Hart, "Definition and Theory in Jurisprudence", *Essays in Jurisprudence and Philosophy* (Oxford University Press 1984) 17.

[6] See e.g. Paddy Ireland, "Limited Liability, Shareholder Rights and the Problem of Corporate Irresponsibility" (2010) 34 Cambridge Journal of Economics 837.

[7] See e.g. Craig M Kauffman and Pamela L Martin, *The Politics of Rights of Nature: Strategies for Building a More Sustainable Future* (MIT Press 2021); Erin L O'Donnell and Julia Talbot-Jones, "Creating Legal Rights for Rivers: Lessons from Australia, New Zealand, and India" (2018) 23 Ecology and Society 7.

to some broader notion of personhood. The latter half of the Element will focus on particular types of legal persons. Section 3 will focus on the "classical" categories of natural persons (human beings) and artificial persons (corporations). Section 4, on the other hand, will discuss three emerging categories of legal persons: animals, nature and natural objects, and AI systems.

1 What Is Legal Personhood?

The notion of legal personhood is fraught with ambiguity. It not only has a long history within the law, but personhood as a more general concept is important outside of law as well. Furthermore, the notions of being a *person* and a *subject* are interconnected, and the two terms are in certain cases used in closely related ways.

Legal personhood pertains to how one is viewed or treated by the law. However, "person" and "personhood" are often invoked outside of legal contexts. In ethics, *moral persons* are entities that have a central status in morality. Often, the phrase "moral person" is taken to be more or less synonymous with "moral agent", referring to an entity with the capacity to act in accordance with morality and respond to and deliberate upon moral reasons. However, some scholars also use the term to refer to (some) *moral patients*: beings that are not moral agents but that are regardless morally considerable, that is, that they matter morally in their own right.[8] The term "subject" is occasionally used in these contexts as well. Tom Regan has famously argued that being a "subject-of -a-life" – consisting of capacities such as memory, sense of the future, welfare interests, and so on – is a sufficient condition for moral status.[9] Another philosophical context where the term "person" is often invoked is metaphysics. Here, the problem of defining personhood is connected to issues dealing with personal identity, such as whether – and under what conditions – we can say that a 10-year-old John Smith is the same person as a 70-year-old John Smith. Metaphysical accounts of personhood often define personhood more broadly, without necessarily trying to draw any moral conclusions, such as that all persons would be morally considerable.[10] However, the concepts do of course overlap to a high extent, and a metaphysical person can very well meet the

---

[8] For an overview of how personhood and moral status could be interrelated, see Mary Anne Warren, *Moral Status: Obligations to Persons and Other Living Things* (Oxford University Press 1997) Chapter 4.

[9] Tom Regan, *The Case for Animal Rights* (University of California Press 2004).

[10] For instance, Christian List and Philip Pettit argue that organised human collectivities can be seen as persons. However, they do not make an argument for the moral considerability of such collectivites. See Christopher List and Philip Pettit, *Group Agency: The Possibility, Design, and Status of Corporate Agents* (Oxford University Press 2011).

criteria of moral personhood as well. Often, scholars discuss personhood *simpliciter*, that is, without specifying whether they are referring to moral or metaphysical – or legal – personhood. In such cases, they often implicitly mean either moral or metaphysical personhood, or some "mix" of the two.

Let us now move to legal personhood specifically. Even in this relatively narrow context, there are a number of different approaches that do not always easily converse with each other. First, we need to disambiguate three different ways in which legal personhood/subjecthood is approached by scholars. When discussing legal personhood or subjecthood, we may be referring to at least three different things: (1) a legal-conceptual scheme, (2) certain presuppositions made by a legal system or an area of law, or (3) a subjectifying practice.

First, "legal personhood" can refer to a legal-conceptual scheme, used in Western law to make sense of and categorise legal materials and norms. Some entities are legal persons or subjects, whereas others are legal nonpersons, "things", or objects. Legal persons have a particular legal status, and under this approach, the focus is on analysing what this status means. How would animals' legal status be different if they were legal persons? Should some AI systems be afforded legal personhood?

Second, when discussing personhood in a legal context, we can refer to a set of presuppositions that a legal system or an area of law makes about, typically, human beings. A quotation from Michael Moore should exemplify this approach pithily: "Once one sees that criminal law presuppose[s] that those subject to it must at least be rational agents [. . .] the question arises as to what other fundamental attributes the law might suppose persons to have".[11]

Finally, we can discern an approach to personhood/subjecthood that is close to the second one just outlined, but still subtly different. Here the focus is not on what the law presupposes but rather on how it may construe subjectivities. This approach is strongly influenced by Michel Foucault's thought. For instance, a criminal justice system creates power relationships between individuals and the state, and individuals come to internalise (i.e. accept and adopt) the values embedded in the legal system. This process Foucault calls "subjectification".[12] This approach is employed and aptly described in Susanna Lindroos-Hovinheimo's book addressing legal personhood under the European Union privacy protection regime. She takes her key question to be: "What kind of persons does European Union (EU) law think we are?". But she takes

---

[11] Michael S Moore, *Placing Blame: A Theory of the Criminal Law* (Oxford University Press 2010) Chapter 15, abstract.

[12] See Michel Foucault, *Discipline and Punish* (Allen Lane tr, Penguin Books 1977). See also Todd May, "Subjectification" in Leonard Lawlor and John Nale (eds), *The Cambridge Foucault Lexicon* (1st ed., Cambridge University Press 2014) 496.

a Foucauldian approach by adopting the hypothesis that "there is no subject prior to social, economic, political and legal conditions". Instead, she "display[s] the person with privacy rights, that is, the private person, as constructed" and asks: "What if a private person never existed as such but was drafted, recognised and created in various practices and counter-practices, of which the most important have been legal?".[13]

These three different approaches are of course not mutually exclusive. For instance, one may simultaneously investigate the legal-conceptual scheme of legal personhood and its underlying assumptions about human beings.

The rest of this Element is primarily focused on legal personhood in the first sense: as a legal-conceptual scheme. I take this understanding of legal personhood to be the primary one in legal contexts, and it is this notion of legal personhood that is invoked when the legal personhood of animals, AI, nature, and so and are discussed.

What kind of a conceptual scheme is legal personhood, then? We can distinguish at least four central questions pertaining to legal personhood:

(1) What does it mean to be a legal person?
(2) Which entities are legal persons?
(3) Which entities can be legal persons?
(4) Which entities should be legal persons?[14]

This section is primarily focused on answering question (1). I will shortly present the Orthodox View, which I take to the primary example of a *formal* account of legal personhood. After that, I will present my own Bundle Theory of legal personhood as an example of a *substantive* view.

As regards question (2), the short answer is this: Western legal systems are relatively unified in what entities they treat as legal persons. There are two central categories. The most central is so-called *natural persons*, meaning born human individuals. Some natural persons, such as adults deemed to be of sound mind, are *active legal persons*, meaning that the law treats them as agents: they can decide about their own affairs and be held responsible. Other natural persons, such as infants, are *passive legal persons*: they need others to

---

[13] Susanna Lindroos-Hovinheimo, *Private Selves: Legal Personhood in European Privacy Protection* (Cambridge University Press 2021) 34.

[14] Claudio Novelli, Giorgio Bongiovanni and Giovanni Sartor distinguish between three types of questions pertaining to legal personhood: "(1) Under what conditions is an entity considered a person in law (*trigger conditions*)? (2) What consequences follow from having personality (*legal implications*)? (3) What set of facts explains/justifies why the trigger conditions activate the legal justifications (*background reasons*)?" Claudio Novelli, Giorgio Bongiovanni and Giovanni Sartor, "A Conceptual Framework for Legal Personality and Its Application to AI" (2022) 13 Jurisprudence 194, 204.

administer their rights and are not held responsible for their actions. The other central category of legal persons is that of *artificial* (or *juristic*) *persons*, comprising limited liability companies, states and so on. Further to these main categories, one might argue that at least some natural entities have already been endowed with legal personhood, and that some nonhuman animals have at least received some rights typically associated with legal personhood. These questions will be further explored in Sections 3 and 4. Questions (3) and (4), on the other hand, will be explored in Section 2.

Definitions of Legal Personhood: The Orthodox View

What salient feature distinguishes legal persons from legal nonpersons? Until recently, virtually all scholars and jurists have answered this question along the lines of what I have termed the *Orthodox View of legal personhood.*

The Orthodox View can be described as a "formal" or "thin" understanding of legal personhood, as opposed to a "substantive" or "thick" view.[15] For instance, according to one version of the Orthodox View, one is a legal person if one holds *any* legal right or duty. Hence, the fact that some X is a legal person tells relatively little about X's legal situation. On the other hand, according to a substantive view, not any right or duty will suffice for the status of a legal person; rather, one must hold a more specific legal status to qualify as a legal person. For example, according to Jonas-Sébastien Beaudry, legal personhood is associated with "a plethora of the most robust kinds of protections and rights".[16]

The Orthodox View in fact comprises a number of views that define legal personhood in highly similar ways. According to some of the most important formulations of the Orthodox View, some X is a legal person if and only if:

(1a) X holds legal rights or bears legal duties (*Rights-or-Duties View*),

(1b) X holds legal rights and bears legal duties (*Rights-and-Duties View*),

(2) X has the capacity to hold rights and/or bear legal duties (*Capacity-for-Rights View*),

(3) X is a bundle of legal rights and/or duties (*Legal-Persons-as-Rights-and-Duties* View)[17]

---

[15] This thin/thick terminology is inspired by Novelli, Bongiovanni and Sartor (n 14). This is not to say that all formal views would necessarily fall under the Orthodox View. One could have a definition of legal personhood that is formal but makes no reference to rights or duties (or to legal relations).

[16] Jonas-Sébastien Beaudry, "From Autonomy to Habes Corpus: Animal Rights Activists Take the Parameters of Legal Personhood to Court" (2016) Global Journal of Animal Law 3, 5.

[17] See Visa AJ Kurki, *A Theory of Legal Personhood* (Oxford University Press 2019) Chapter 2.

We can classify versions of the Orthodox View into three main groups. According to the first two versions, the holding of rights and/or duties directly entails legal personhood. However, according to the Rights-and-Duties View, one must hold both rights *and* duties in order to qualify as a legal person, whereas according to the Rights-or-Duties View, it is sufficient to hold merely rights (or duties). In a 2014 chimpanzee rights case, a New York court claimed that "legal personhood has consistently been defined in terms of both rights and duties". It then argued that chimpanzees' "incapability to bear any legal responsibilities and societal duties [. . .] renders it inappropriate to confer upon chimpanzees the legal rights [. . .] that have been afforded to human beings".[18] The plaintiff organisation, the Nonhuman Rights Project, has been critical of this judgment, noting for instance that many of the scholars cited by the court actually explicitly endorse the Rights-or-Duties View.[19] The Rights-and-Duties View has also the unpalatable conclusion that certain human beings, such as infants and young children, are not legal persons (assuming that they cannot bear legal responsibilities).

Adherents of the Capacity-for-Rights View, on the other hand, understand legal personhood as a precondition for rights: one cannot hold rights unless one has been bestowed with legal personhood. Thus, for instance, slaves under antebellum US law lacked the capacity for rights, meaning that they could not for example enter into legally enforceable contracts.[20] This definition of legal personhood is particularly dominant in the civil-law tradition, where the notion of "legal capacity" (*Rechtsfähigkeit, capacité juridique, capacidad jurídica*) can even be found in some private-law codifications. However, the English terminology here is highly ambiguous, which will necessitate a brief diversion. First, as traditionally understood in the civil-law tradition, "legal capacity" is a part of what I term passive legal personhood, which does not require any kind of agency: even infants have legal capacity. However, the term has become ambiguous because "legal capacity" is in certain contexts – especially in disability law – also used to describe the legal empowerment to make decisions about one's affairs, which is a part of active legal

---

[18] *People ex rel. Nonhuman Rights Project, Inc.* v. *Lavery* 2014 NY Slip Op 08531 Decided on 4 December 2014 Appellate Division, Third Department Peters, J.

[19] Steven M Wise, "A New York Appellate Court Takes a First Swing at Chimpanzee Personhood and Misses" (2017) 95 Denver Law Review 265, 278–9.

[20] Kaarlo Tuori offers a distinct version of the Capacity-For-Rights position: "All sociolegal roles share a common basic presupposition. One cannot be employer or employee, landlord or tenant, consumer or CEO, president or minister without being a legal subject and possessing legal capacity. Legal subjectivity [. . .] is a prerequisite for occupying distinct sociolegal roles; a meta-role, if you want". (Kaarlo Tuori, *Properties of Law: Modern Law and after* (Cambridge University Press 2021) 79.) This view suffers from similar problems as the Capacity-for-Rights view in general. For instance, is being a slave not a sociolegal role?

personhood.[21] Sometimes the phrase denotes some aspects of both active and passive legal personhood.[22] (These developments in disability law will be discussed further in Section 3.) Given the ambiguity of these terms, I have opted for the phrases "passive legal personhood" and "active legal personhood", which I take to be relatively unambiguous.[23]

The final view listed above – the Legal-Persons-as-Rights-and-Duties View – is somewhat different from the rest: it identifies the legal person not as a subject of rights and/or duties, but as the rights and/or duties themselves – as what I will, in Section 2, term the *legal platform*. Hans Kelsen was probably the most stringent adherent of the view according to which a legal person is simply rights and duties. He wrote:

> Man [i.e. human being] is a concept of biology and physiology, in short, of the natural sciences. Person is a concept of jurisprudence, of the analysis of legal norms.
>
> That man and person are two entirely different concepts may be regarded as a generally accepted result of analytical jurisprudence. Only, one does not always draw therefrom the last consequence. This consequence is that the physical (natural) person as the *subject of duties and rights is not the human being whose conduct is the contents of these duties or the object of these rights* [...].[24]

Hence, for Kelsen, there are two concepts: human being and (legal) person. A human being is flesh and blood, belonging to the world of "is", whereas a person is simply an array of rights and duties that can be attributed to the human being. Persons thus belong to the world of "ought". The person is not, according to Kelsen, a human being *qua* right-holder and duty-bearer. Rather, the person simply is the rights and duties that can be imputed to the human being.

---

[21] This usage is most apparent in the Convention on the Rights of Persons with Disabilities. Article 12 (1–2) of the Convention states that "States Parties reaffirm that persons with disabilities have the right to recognition everywhere as persons before the law" and that "States Parties shall recognise that persons with disabilities enjoy legal capacity on an equal basis with others in all aspects of life". (Convention on the Rights of Persons with Disabilities, adopted on 13 December 2006; entered into force on 3 May 2008.) Here, being a *person before the law* means passive legal personhood, whereas *legal capacity* refers to an incident of active legal personhood: what I call "legal competence", i.e. being empowered to decide about one's own affairs.

[22] Amita Dhanda, "Legal Capacity in the Disability Rights Convention: Stranglehold of the Past or Lodestar for the Future" (2007) 34 Syracuse Journal of International Law and Commerce 429, 442–3; Anna Nilsson, "Who Gets to Decide? Right to Legal Capacity for Persons with Intellectual and Psychosocial Disabilities" (Council of Europe Commissioner for Human Rights 2012) 9–10 https://wcd.coe.int/ViewDoc.jsp?p=&id=1908555&direct=true; Anna Arstein-Kerslake, *Legal Capacity & Gender: Realising the Human Right to Legal Personhood and Agency of Women, Disabled Women, and Gender Minorities* (Springer 2021) 1–28.

[23] The passive/active terminology is inspired by Neil MacCormick. See Neil MacCormick, *Institutions of Law: An Essay in Legal Theory* (Oxford University Press 2007).

[24] Hans Kelsen, *General Theory of Law and State* (Transaction 2006) 94, emphasis added.

The Orthodox View and Theories of Rights

All versions of the Orthodox View need to be augmented by some account of the notions of right and duty. Both are thorny concepts, but the notion of rights in particular has been vigorously contested. Especially in the English-speaking world, a typical starting point when theorising about rights is the analysis introduced by Wesley Newcomb Hohfeld.[25] Hohfeld noted that the term "right" and other cognate terms are used in various, subtly different ways. For instance, it is normal to think that rights and duties are closely connected. However, there seem to be situations where we talk about rights without such a connection. We can say that Jane has the right to look at her neighbour's garden from her house. Regardless, the neighbour is under no duty to allow this; he can for instance block Jane's view by installing a tall fence. Hence, when we talk about Jane's right here, we mean that Jane is *permitted* to view her neighbour's garden. Hohfeld called such permissions *privileges*, and they are today usually called *liberties* or *liberty-rights*. On the other hand, *claim-rights* are rights that are correlated by duties. They are usually understood as the most central case of rights, and some scholars think that the word "right" should be reserved exclusively for claim-rights. However, the nature of claim-rights is not obvious.

Two main theories seek to explain what it means to hold a (claim-)right: the will theory and the interest theory. According to the *will theory*, holding a right means being empowered to make legally enforceable choices over the duties of others.[26] For instance, if Maria owes some money to Ali, the latter has a right in this situation because he can for instance demand that Maria pay the debt, or choose to waive it. It is his choice. On the other hand, according to the *interest theory*, one holds a right if one's interests are served by the duty of someone. Under the interest theory, Ali holds a right in the scenario as well, but for a different reason: because receiving money is, typically, in his interests (i.e. good for him). These theories come apart when we consider more controversial topics, such as animal rights. Many will theorists would claim that nonhuman animals cannot hold rights because they cannot, for instance, demand their rights, whereas animal rights are easier to explain under the interest theory: animals – at least sentient animals – certainly have interests, such as the interest not to suffer pain.[27]

---

[25] Wesley Newcomb Hohfeld, "Some Fundamental Legal Conceptions as Applied in Legal Reasoning" (1913) 23 Yale Law Journal 16.

[26] I am here talking about "others" for the sake of simplicity, but I am not ruling out the possibility that one could hold rights towards oneself.

[27] See e.g. Matthew H Kramer, NE Simmonds, and Hillel Steiner, *A Debate over Rights. Philosophical Enquiries* (Oxford University Press 1998); Joel Feinberg, "The Rights of Animals and Unborn Generations" in William T Blackstone (ed), *Philosophy and Environmental Crisis* (The University of Georgia Press 1974); Matthew H Kramer, "Do Animals and Dead People Have Legal Rights?" (2001) 14 Canadian Journal of Law & Jurisprudence 29; Saskia Stucki, "Towards

The import of these theories for the discussion over legal personhood is not as straightforward as one might think. I will mention three issues here. First, one may ask whether any Hohfeldian legal position (such as a liberty) is enough to make its holder count as a legal person on the Orthodox View, or whether only claim-rights count.[28] Second, one might think that the theories of rights also limit who or what can be a legal person: for instance, if one adheres to the will theory, one will plausibly deny that animals can hold rights or be legal persons. Hence – and assuming that animals cannot bear duties, either – animals cannot be legal persons. However, many people writing on legal personhood would, in fact, deny this conclusion. Instead, many subscribe to what I term the "Anything-Goes View": legal personhood can be given to (virtually) anything. I will address this view in Section 2. Second, the Capacity-for-Rights View can easily be misunderstood. Philosophers or rights theorists might understand the "capacity for rights" as the capacity to hold rights in general.[29] Hence, for instance, adult human beings of sound mind would be a paradigmatic example of someone with a capacity for rights, whereas nonhuman animals would not have the capacity for rights under the will theory. Such capacity does not depend on legal decisions; elsewhere, I have denoted it the "conceptual capacity for rights".[30] However, this is not how the "capacity for rights" is typically understood in the legal personhood context. Rather, the capacity for rights is understood as a legal status, whereby the legal system treats someone as a potential right-holder.

The Orthodox Inventory and Its History

The Orthodox View is part of a broader "Orthodox Inventory of the Universe" (Figure 1. This inventory divides the world into two categories: persons (subjects) and things (objects). This division is understood to be of the highest level (*summa divisio*) and exhaustive (*tertium non datur*; "there is no third"). If one accepts such an Orthodox Inventory, one must also accept a formal definition of legal thinghood: everything that is not a legal person, is a legal thing.[31]

---

a Theory of Legal Animal Rights: Simple and Fundamental Rights" (2020) 40 Oxford Journal of Legal Studies 533.

[28] I have elsewhere labelled the idea that any Hohfeldian position would be sufficient for legal personhood as the "Capacity-for-Legal-Relations position". This position is untenable; see Kurki, *A Theory of Legal Personhood* (n 17) 83–6.

[29] What I mean by "conceptual capacity" is what Joshua Gellers means by "capacity", even if he notes the distinction between conceptual and legal capacity. Joshua C Gellers, *Rights for Robots: Artificial Intelligence, Animal and Environmental Law* (Routledge 2020) 154.

[30] See Visa AJ Kurki, "Legal Power and Legal Competence" in Mark McBride (ed), *New Essays on the Nature of Rights* (Hart 2017).

[31] Whether the Orthodox Inventory truly covers "everything" can be questioned. There may be different ontological views as to "what there is". One who accepts the Orthodox Inventory might, for instance, claim that it only covers concrete and not abstract objects, or at least not all abstract

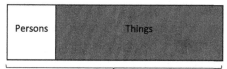

Figure 1 The Orthodox Inventory of the universe. Persons hold rights
and/or duties, or the capacity to hold rights/duties. Everything else
falls under things

The history of the Orthodox View is often understood to date back to Roman law
and the works of the jurisconsult Gaius. However, this is most likely
a misconception. Gaius did indeed divide his *Institutes* (*Institutiones*) into three
parts, addressing persons, things and actions.[32] But it is unlikely that he would have
meant this pedagogical division as presenting three, mutually exclusive categories.
The "law of persons", for instance, does not address whether one is a person or not,
but rather the law of personal statuses: whether one is Roman or non-Roman, head
of the family or not, and so on. Another telling example is slaves: though typically
understood as paradigmatic examples of human beings who are not legal persons
but rather things, Gaius mentioned slaves under both persons and things.[33]

Rather than truly dating back to Roman law and Gaius, the Orthodox Inventory
can be understood as a product of modern-era legal scholarship, starting with
Renaissance Humanists such as Hugues Doneau (Hugo Donellus, 1527–91) and
developed further by Continental European legal scholars. The idea of personhood and thinghood as strictly mutually exclusive categories was prominent in
the legal and moral philosophies of Immanuel Kant and GWF Hegel, and the
most prominent legal-doctrinal expression of this idea was likely by the great
German legal scholar Friedrich Carl von Savigny. These Continental ideas were
imported to the Anglophone world by the great English legal philosopher John
Austin, who had studied at the University of Bonn, Germany.[34]

Criticism of the Orthodox View

Though the Orthodox View is the prevalent way of understanding legal personhood, it can be criticised. Let us now consider some problems of the view.

---

objects. See José L Falguera, Concha Martínez-Vidal and Gideon Rosen, "Abstract Objects" in
Edward N Zalta (ed), *The Stanford Encyclopedia of Philosophy* (Metaphysics Research Lab,
Stanford University 2022) https://plato.stanford.edu/archives/sum2022/entries/abstract-objects/
accessed 19 December 2022.

[32] Gaius, *Institutiones or Institutes of Roman Law* (Edward Poste tr ed., 4th ed., Clarendon Press
1904).

[33] See PW Duff, *Personality in Roman Private Law* (Cambridge University Press 1938).

[34] See Kurki, *A Theory of Legal Personhood* (n 17) Chapter 1.

The first problem has to do with *simplistic nature*. Though simplicity is of course a desideratum of a theory, it should not come at the cost of explanatory power. For instance, the Orthodox View struggles at explaining *grey areas*, such as the just-mentioned legal status of slaves, who were legal nonpersons for most purposes, but persons for the purposes of being liable under criminal law; and *gradual changes*, such as the steady progress of women towards full legal personhood.

A somewhat more complex issue has to do with what may be termed the *discrepancy problem*.[35] The Orthodox View leads to contradictions if we combine it with (1) typical modern theories of rights and (2) certain widely accepted *extensional beliefs*, that is, beliefs regarding who or what is a legal person. For instance, nonhuman animals today, and slaves in the antebellum US, are both typically classified as legal nonpersons. However, it is highly plausible to think that animals hold, and slaves held, rights. Nonhuman animals are protected in ways that are quite straightforwardly classifiable as rights under the interest theory of rights – though these protections only meet the criteria for "simple rights" rather than "fundamental rights", under the taxonomy of Saskia Stucki.[36] Slaves were protected in similar ways, but they also held some legal positions classifiable as rights under the will theory, such as the right to appeal criminal convictions.[37] Hence, the Orthodox View, modern theories of rights and said extensional beliefs are incompatible.

The Capacity-for-Rights view, in particular, suffers from problems having to do with its origins in private-law theory. The notion of giving some X the "capacity for rights and duties" has explanatory power within private law: private law has to do with setting up a framework where individuals and other actors can acquire rights and duties as a result of transactions and delicts. However, this idea of a capacity for rights does not make as much sense outside of private law. For instance, if we take certain criminalisations – such as the crimes of battery and murder – to entail rights (as the interest theory would have it[38]) then the legislator needs to simply enact such criminalisations in order to give these kinds of rights to X. There is no need for a separate declaration that X "can hold rights within criminal law"; such declarations are superfluous. Some other declarations – such as endowing X with legal standing and the status of a criminal-law victim – are of course meaningful, but merely conferring upon

---

[35] See ibid 14–16.

[36] Stucki (n 27). Clare McCausland, "The Five Freedoms of Animal Welfare Are Rights" (2014) 27 Journal of Agricultural and Environmental Ethics 649–62.

[37] See Visa AJ Kurki, *A Theory of Legal Personhood* (Oxford University Press 2019) 68; Judith Kelleher Schafer, "Long Arm of the Law: Slave Criminals and the Supreme Court in Antebellum Louisiana" (1985) 60 Tulane Law Review 1247.

[38] Rights can result from criminalisations under the will theory as well, but this presupposes the capacity to waive the criminal-law protection.

them the "capacity for rights" is not. Conceptualising legal personhood merely in terms of the capacity for rights would also lead to some strange consequences. Let us suppose that Solveig could enter contracts and own property, but that anyone could also freely hit or kill her without any consequences. It would at least be somewhat strange to label her a legal person. It is more plausible to understand legal personhood as partly about the "capacity" for certain rights and/or duties, but partly as the actual holding of certain rights and/or duties.

Substantive Views and the Bundle Theory of Legal Personhood

Though prevalent, the Orthodox View is not the only option. Some scholars have offered alternatives, though most of them have not presented an overall account of legal personhood. For instance, Jonas-Sébastien Beaudry has described legal personhood as a "golden ticket" and distinguished it from granting weak rights to some entity, whereas Tomasz Pietrzykowski has distinguished legal personhood from the status of "non-personal subjects of law".[39] I have offered a book-length argument against the Orthodox View, arguing instead for a substantive, or "thick", view of legal personhood.[40] Given that my theory is, to my knowledge, the only thoroughly developed alternative to the Orthodox View, I will now present it in some depth.

According to my Bundle Theory, legal personhood functions somewhat like ownership: it consists of *incidents of legal personhood*, which together form a bundle. Very roughly put, I have argued that legal persons are characterised not by the fact that they hold any rights at all, but rather by the fact that they hold a large number of rights (and duties) – that is, incidents of legal personhood.[41] One can hold some legal rights without being a legal person. Legal thinghood, on the other hand, is best understood as being the (potential) object of property rights, that is, the susceptibility to being owned.[42] The most prominent explanation of property rights (ownership), on the other hand, explains it in terms of a bundle of rights (and duties).[43] Both legal personhood and thinghood are best

---

[39] Beaudry (n 16); Tomasz Pietrzykowski, "The Idea of Non-Personal Subjects of Law" in Visa AJ Kurki and Tomasz Pietrzykowski (eds), *Legal Personhood: Animals, Artificial Intelligence and the Unborn* (Springer 2017).

[40] Kurki, *A Theory of Legal Personhood* (n 17).

[41] ibid. Strictly put, whether all of the incidents of legal personhood can be described in terms of rights and duties depends on one's theory of rights. The most important building blocks of these incidents are claim-rights, duties, and competences. However, I have here opted for the more straightforward language of rights and duties.

[42] Visa AJ Kurki, "Animals, Slaves and Corporations: Analyzing Legal Thinghood" (2017) 18 German Law Journal 1096.

[43] Anthony M Honoré, "Ownership" in AG Guest (ed), *Oxford Essays in Jurisprudence* (Oxford University Press 1961); Shane Nicholas Glackin, "Back to Bundles: Deflating Property Rights, Again" (2014) 20 Legal Theory 1.

Table 1 The incidents of legal personhood

Passive incidents of legal personhood		Active incidents of legal personhood	
Substantive passive incidents	*Remedy incidents*	*Legal competences*	*Onerous legal personhood*
– fundamental protections: protection of life, liberty, and bodily integrity – capacity to be the beneficiary of special rights – capacity to own property – insusceptibility to being owned	– standing in courts and other officials – victim status in criminal law – capacity to undergo legal harms	Capacity to administer the other incidents without a representative, for example the capacity to enter into contracts	Legal responsibility in criminal law, tort law and other contexts

understood as cluster properties, that is, both can be explained in terms of bundles of rights and duties, not all of which need to be present in order for an instance of a legal person or a thing to be present.

The incidents of legal personhood are laid out in Table 1. The incidents are disseverable, and one does not need to hold all of these rights and duties in order to qualify as a legal person, at least for some limited purposes. Legal personhood is therefore a cluster property. Nonetheless, the central types of legal persons – such as natural persons and corporations – hold all, or the vast majority, of these incidents. The incidents are divided into passive and active.[44] The passive incidents do not presuppose the capacity for sophisticated action, which is why even human infants may be endowed with them. Adult human beings, on the other hand, are normally endowed also with the active incidents.

Passive legal personhood consists of the kind of incidents that infants are endowed with in a typical Western legal system. Compare a human infant with, say, a nonhuman animal. Nonhuman animals are not legal persons in typical Western legal systems, even if animal welfare legislation protects them from some forms of maltreatment. On the other hand, a human infant – let us call her

---

[44] This passive/active terminology is inspired by Neil MacCormick's treatment in MacCormick (n 23).

Mari – is endowed with the whole array of passive incidents of legal personhood. These incidents fall under two groups. The *substantive incidents* determine Mari's "primary" rights vis-à-vis others and the state. These include her being endowed with strong protections that pertain to her life, liberty and bodily integrity; the fact that contracts can be entered in her name; her being able to own property; and her insusceptibility to being owned. The *remedy incidents*, on the other hand, determine what legal means Mari (or rather her representative, on her behalf) can resort to if her substantive incidents are not respected. Say that someone infringes upon Mari's right to bodily integrity.[45] The harm Mari has undergone may be given legal recognition, meaning that the tortfeasor – the one who committed the harm – may be liable to compensate Mari. The latter also has legal standing, meaning that the tortfeasor can be sued in her name. Finally, if the infringement of her rights is serious enough, she may also be deemed the victim of a crime. Thus, not only does Mari enjoy much stronger protections than virtually all nonhuman animals, but she also has access to legal personhood-related tools that are usually unavailable to animals, such as legal standing and tort law.

Let us then consider *active legal personhood*. Compare Mari with Solveig, who is an adult and *sui iuris*, that is, not under the power of another. Solveig's situation is different in at least two regards. First, Solveig may administer her own rights and duties; she normally does not require a representative. Second, Solveig may be held legally responsible in various ways. She is thus endowed with not only passive but also active legal personhood. This aspect of legal personhood requires a certain degree of agency: for instance, the capacity to operate with notions such as contracts requires some understanding of the legal-normative world. I will discuss certain aspects of the passive/active distinction more carefully below.

If one accepts the Bundle Theory – or at least rejects the Orthodox View – one may also reconsider the Orthodox Inventory. I would instead argue for a Substantive Inventory, according to which legal personhood and legal thinghood are not formal, but rather substantive categories. X's status as a person or a thing depends on much more than merely whether X holds at least one right; it is rather connected to one's legal situation in multifarious ways. Furthermore, the person/thing bifurcation is not exhaustive: there may be entities that are neither persons nor things. A classical example would be outlawry, an institution prevalent at least in medieval England and Sweden: an outlaw was banished from the society and stripped of rights, but they did not

---

[45] I am here assuming that passive legal personhood entails rights, an assumption that may be contested by will theorists of rights. They are free to replace the label "right" with a term of their choosing.

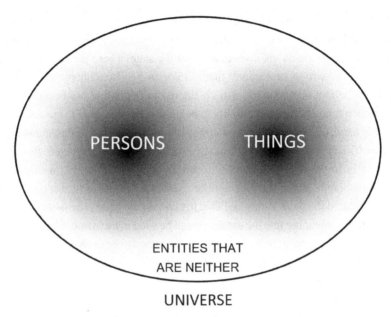

Figure 2 The Substantive Inventory. Both personhood are thinghood are cluster properties, with no clear borders. Furthermore, one may even be a person *and* a thing to a limited extent, and also an entity that is neither a person nor a thing

become things either – they could not legally be owned. The Substantive Inventory is presented in Figure 2.

Weaknesses and Criticism the Bundle Theory

The Bundle Theory and substantive views more generally do also have weaknesses vis-à-vis the Orthodox View. Most importantly, the Orthodox View is straightforward to understand and explain, whereas substantive views need to explain the difference between being a right-holder and a legal person.[46] Scholars have also proposed new formulations of the Orthodox View to counter some of the criticisms levelled against it while retaining its simplicity. For instance, Raffael Fasel has argued that legal personhood could be explained as the holding of fundamental (rather than any) rights.[47]

---

[46] Now, even though the Bundle Theory is considerably more complex, its main features can also be explained in relatively straightforward terms. The basic idea can be summarised non-rigorously as follows: Legal personhood is not about *whether* one holds rights and/or duties, but about *how many* and *what kind of* rights and/or duties one holds. Rather than holding simply any rights at all, legal persons hold many rights and, potentially, duties.

[47] Raffael N Fasel, "Shaving Ockham: A Review of Visa A. J. Kurki's 'A Theory of Legal Personhood'" (2021) 44 Revus 113–26.

The Orthodox View is also simpler in setting relatively clear boundaries between legal persons and nonpersons, as opposed to the Bundle Theory, which explains legal personhood as a cluster property with fuzzy boundaries.

Another strength of the Orthodox View has to do with civil-law terminology. Civilian jurisdictions typically employ as synonyms of "legal person" terms that can be translated into English as "legal subject" or "subject of law", but also as "subject of right(s)".[48] Under this terminology, the Orthodox View makes much more sense, because according to the Orthodox View, the legal person is simply a subject of rights (and duties). Inspired by Tomasz Pietrzykowski, I have sought to address this issue by distinguishing between "legal person" and "legal subject", which I will discuss this next.[49]

Legal Subjecthood

In a general sense, all entities that hold rights and/or duties in a legal system are legal subjects *tout court* ("without qualifications"). Hence, for instance, animals are already legal subjects in those jurisdictions where they are protected in a manner that confers upon them rights. However, legal subjecthood can also meaningfully be approached in terms of areas of law, or legal institutions. For instance, to generalise greatly, corporations are in Europe typically not subjects of fundamental rights law, whereas natural persons are. Legal personhood can be seen as consisting of having a specific subject status in various areas of law.

I take legal subjecthood to be analysable in terms of two pairs of categories: substantive/procedural and passive/active.[50] A relatively simple example is provided in Table 2.

As with legal personhood, we can again compare the infant Mari with the adult Solveig. First, Mari can be party to a contract (passive–substantive), and to a lawsuit pertaining to the contract (passive–procedural). If she incurs contractual duties, she will not be required to carry them out personally; rather, her representative is expected to take care of this. Mari is therefore a passive subject of contract law. On the other hand, Solveig can decide which contracts to enter into. She can also decide to sue over a contract, and she must fulfil the ensuing duties personally unless she has delegated the responsibility. Solveig is therefore also an active subject of contract law. Now contrast both Mari and Solveig with nonhuman animals, who are neither passive nor active subjects of contract law. Not only are animals unable to make legal decisions pertaining

---

[48] E.g. *Rechtssubjekt, sujet de droit and sujeto de derecho(s)*.

[49] See Pietrzykowski (n 39). See also SM Solaiman, "Legal Personality of Robots, Corporations, Idols and Chimpanzees: A Quest for Legitimacy" (2017) 25 Artificial Intelligence and Law 155.

[50] For a good analysis, see Alf Ross, *On Law and Justice* (Jakob vH Holtermann ed., Uta Binreiter tr, Oxford University Press 2019) 216–19.

Table 2 Subjecthood under contract law

	Passive subjecthood	**Active subjecthood**
Substantive aspect	Capacity to be party to a contract.	Legal competence to enter contracts oneself; capacity to bear contract-law duties
Procedural aspect	Capacity to be party to a lawsuit over contract.	Legal competence to, for example, choose to sue in order to enforce the contract

to contracts – they cannot be parties to contracts at all (nor to lawsuits over contracts).[51]

In an analysis of Finnish criminal law, I have detected a somewhat more nuanced structure of subjecthood, which I take to consist of six different categories (see Table 3). Let us consider the substantive aspect first. *Protectees* are the entities whose interests are protected by criminal law in a way that entails interest-theory rights.[52] Being a protectee does not presuppose agency, and falls therefore under passive subjecthood. Under active-substantive subjecthood we find two distinct categories: the capacity to commit crimes, that is, being criminally liable, and the competence to consent to acts that would otherwise – without the consent – be crimes.

As regards the procedural aspect, we can find two passive categories and one active category. The passive categories include procedural victim status – in Nordic law "the one who owns the case", with associated rights and competences[53] – and the capacity to be the suspect or defendant of criminal proceedings. Classifying the latter category as passive may strike some as surprising. However, the liability to be convicted of crimes is not, under Finnish law, precluded by the defendant's unsound mind during the proceedings, as long as they were of sound mind when committing the crime. Finally, the active-procedural aspect has to do with whether one can make decisions in various legal procedures: only active-procedural subjects can, for instance, demand punishment on their own (as victims). However, even active-procedural subjects may,

---

[51] One might argue that so-called pet trusts might entail passive contractual subjecthood for the affected animals. Pet trusts will briefly be discussed in Section 4.

[52] Under Finnish law, I take there to be four categories of protectees: natural persons, artificial persons, foetuses, and nonhuman animals.

[53] This status does not always coincide with the victim of the crime; in the case of homicides, certain family members of the victim are typically seen as the "ones who own the case".

Table 3 Subjecthood under Finnish criminal law.

	Passive subjecthood	Active subjecthood
Substantive aspect	Having one's interests protected by criminalisations (protectee status)	Being potentially liable under criminal law Capacity to consent
Procedural aspect	Capacity for the procedural status of the victim of a crime (Nordic law: "the one who owns the case")	Competence to make decisions in criminal-law proceedings (e.g. demand punishment, plea guilty) Capacity to be suspect or defendant in criminal-law proceedings, and to be convicted of crimes

of course, need a legal counsel representing them, even if the counsel is normally bound by the instructions of their client.[54]

To sum up, if one distinguishes between the legal person and the legal subject, one can find at least a partial compromise between substantive and formal views: substantive views, such as the Bundle Theory, are theories of legal *personhood*, whereas formal views explain the status of being a legal *subject*.

Conclusion

This section has sought to provide an overview of legal personhood, and in particular, what it means to be a legal person. I have first distinguished different meanings of "person" and then focused on the conceptual-scheme understanding of legal personhood. I have then noted that legal personhood can be defined formally or substantively. If defined substantively, it is also possible to distinguish legal personhood from legal subjecthood, where the latter is more clearly a formal property.

The next section will delve deeper into a number of philosophical questions surrounding legal personhood.

2 Legal Personhood as a Conceptual Scheme

This section will be the most theoretical one in nature, addressing some relatively deep philosophical questions underlying legal personhood. I will start by presenting the distinction between realism and legalism about legal personhood, originally introduced by Ngaire Naffine, and develop it further. After that, I will discuss whether anything can be a legal person and who or what should be a legal person. Finally, I will discuss the role of legal personhood in legal reasoning and briefly address whether all systems have legal personhood.

Realism and Legalism

Ngaire Naffine has distinguished two approaches to legal personhood: *realism* and *legalism*. Very roughly put, realists emphasise the connections between legal personhood and other types of personhood, whereas legalists deny or at least downplay those connections. Naffine writes:

> The largest dispute, the biggest intellectual and moral battle, is between those who say that law *does not* and *should not* operate with a natural conception of the person [i.e. legalists], and those who say that it does and should [i.e. realists].[55]

---

[54] See (in Finnish) Visa Kurki, "Rikosoikeuden subjekti" in Esko Yli-Hemminki, Sakari Melander, and Kimmo Nuotio (eds), *Rikoksen ja rangaistuksen filosofia* (Gaudeamus 2023).

[55] Ngaire Naffine, *Law's Meaning of Life: Philosophy, Religion, Darwin and the Legal Person* (Hart 2009) 20.

For Naffine's legalists,

> law is not engaged in [...] metaphysical or natural boundary setting, and so, potentially, law's person has no natural limits. [...] In this orthodox and analytical account of law's person, the defining attributes of a being – its capacity to think or feel or its sanctity – have no direct bearing on whether it has legal personality because the legal person is a construct of law.[56]

Whereas for the realists,

> law should find and reflect its subject which exists beyond law [...] They believe that law finds its subject beyond the legal realm and that law is to be judged by its success at finding and rendering this subject faithfully.[57]

Though an important distinction, I believe the legalism/realism bifurcation contains a number of important subdivisions. I will here divide these into two main categories: the *monism/pluralism* and the *construct/status* distinctions.

Monism and Pluralism

Monist[58] accounts emphasise the connections between personhood *simpliciter* and legal personhood, whereas pluralist accounts emphasise the distinctiveness of legal personhood from personhood. I take most realist accounts to be committed to monism in some form or another. The connection posited by monism can, *prima facie*, be understood in at least three different ways.

First, monism can be understood as a thesis about who or what *can* be a legal person. The most straightforward thesis here would be that persons, and only persons, can be legal persons.

Second, we can take monism to be a thesis about who or what *should* be a legal person. This is how Benjamin Sachs interprets Naffine's realism.[59] Again, the most straightforward way of understanding this thesis would be that persons, and only persons, should be legal persons.

Third, monism can be understood as a conceptual thesis. For instance, Michael Moore seems to think that there is no distinct *legal* personhood at all, but rather simply personhood. He takes personhood in legal contexts to be a "borrowed" concept, though he does not specify what he means by this.[60]

---

[56] ibid 21.   [57] ibid 22.

[58] As is often the case with general scholarly terms, "monism" and "monist" can mean many things. I should note in particular that "monist" here does not mean the same as what Raffael Fasel means by it (in Fasel (n 47)) nor is it identical with how Novelli, Bongiovanni and Sartor use the term in Novelli, Bongiovanni and Sartor (n 14) 206–8.

[59] Benjamin Sachs, *Contractarianism, Role Obligations, and Political Morality* (Routledge 2022) 135–9.

[60] Moore (n 11) 624–5.

According to pluralism, on the other hand, personhood and legal personhood are distinct concepts.

The "can" and "should" questions will be addressed in the sections below, but I will briefly discuss the conceptual thesis here. What exactly does it mean that law would be working with a "borrowed" concept? Law can of course employ non-legal concepts. However, when doing so, the law needs to attach legal consequences that follow if the criteria of the concept obtain. For instance, let us assume that the prohibition of "cruel and unusual punishment" in the US Constitution involves the use of a borrowed moral concept, namely that of CRUEL. However, the legal consequences of when a punishment is deemed cruel and unusual are set out in the law: such punishments are prohibited by the Constitution. The same can be said of (legal) personhood: even if personhood were a borrowed concept within law, the legal consequences of something's being a person would regardless need to be determined. These legal consequences would, then, amount to the status of legal personhood. Regardless, even the status of legal personhood can be derivative from, say, morality. The most straightforward account of such a connection would likely be the following: the status of legal personhood amounts to the legal status that moral persons, according to morality, should have.

Legal Personhood as Status and Construct

Naffine's category of legalism hides yet another conflation. This is apparent in her treatment of Christopher Stone's work. She takes him to be a legalist, and goes on to write:

> Thus he [Stone] is in the same juristic school as Hans Kelsen, for whom '[a] legal person is the unity of a complex of legal obligations and rights. . . . It is not a natural reality but a social construction created by the science of law – an auxiliary concept in the presentation of legally relevant facts'. Legal persons, thus considered, are legal abstractions. They consist of purely legal norms. Legal persons do not have the innate capacity to reason nor do they possess human souls; they do not have arms and legs or bodies, a sex or a species.[61]

Here, we encounter yet another issue underlying the conceptual-scheme understanding of legal personhood: legal personhood can be understood as a status or a construct.

---

[61] Ngaire Naffine, "Legal Personality and the Natural World: On the Persistence of the Human Measure of Value" (2012) 3 Journal of Human Rights and the Environment 68, 82, citing Hans Kelsen, Pure Theory of Law (1934 German ed.) 173–4.

Understood as a *status*, legal personhood is a legal property that attaches to certain entities, of which the paradigmatic example is human beings.[62] Law can give various statuses to human beings, such as that of a husband or a convict. When a slave was freed, his or her legal status was changed from that of a slave (and, subsequently, property) into that of a person.

If legal personhood is understood as a *construct*, legal persons are seen as functioning purely in the legal realm: rather than giving pre-existing entities a legal status, law creates entities.[63] Such an approach to legal personhood finds most appeal when we consider the way corporations and other similar legal arrangements can be created and used in imaginative ways: corporations can create dozens of subsidiaries for tax purposes and transfer assets and liabilities between them at will. Here, new "legal persons" are created, manipulated, and dissolved for various technical reasons. In these kinds of situations, it is tempting to think that nothing "becomes" a legal person when Company Inc. sets up a subsidiary for holding purposes. A legal person appears here as a construct – a legally created entity – rather than as a pre-existing entity newly endowed with a legal status.

I have sought to make sense of this systematically ambiguous[64] nature of legal personhood by distinguishing between a legal person and a legal platform. A legal *person* is an entity that is endowed with the status of legal personhood. Such entities can be individual human beings and human collectivities; and potentially for instance nonhuman animals and robots. A legal *platform*, on the other hand, is merely a legal construct – a bundle of rights and duties with specific features.[65] For every natural person, there is at least one legal platform that attaches to them: for Jane Smith, the platform's name would be "Jane Smith"; it is under this legal

---

[62] I use "status" in the broad sense in which it is used by social ontologists such as John Searle to denote the "social properties" of entities. see John Searle, *Making the Social World: The Structure of Human Civilization* (Oxford University Press 2010).

[63] E.g. FH Lawson, "The Creative Use of Legal Concepts" (1957) 32 New York University Law Review 909.

[64] The phrase "systematically ambiguous" is used in Amin Ebrahimi Afrouzi, "Visa A. J. Kurki, A Theory of Legal Personhood, Oxford: Oxford University Press, 2019, 240 Pp, Hb £ 70.00" (2020) 83 The Modern Law Review 279.

[65] A legal platform has three central features. First, it is *named*, as with "Mary" and "Mary Inc". Second, it is *integrated*: a platform's rights and duties are interconnected in various ways. For instance, Mary Inc. may end up bankrupt because of a loan towards X, which will affect its debts vis-á-vis Y and Z as well. Third, legal platforms are *separate* from each other: Mary's natural legal platform will not directly be affected by the financial liabilities of Mary Inc, as the creditors of Mary Inc. cannot recover from Mary's personal assets. However, the separateness of legal platforms is often a matter of degree. In the case at hand, the separateness is unilateral: the debtors of Mary may typically recover from Mary Inc. because Mary owns Mary Inc. Corporate platforms typically also have a fourth important feature: the individuals to whom they attach can easily change – Mary can sell Mary Inc. anytime she likes. Kurki, *A Theory of Legal Personhood* (n 17) 133–8.

identity that she can operate from cradle to grave. However, in jurisdictions that allow for one-person corporations, she could also set up a separate legal platform, such as "Jane Smith, Inc.". She could then operate under two legal identities. What is distinctive of the latter platform – as is typical of corporate platforms – is that said platform can relatively freely change its object of attachment: Jane can for instance sell her corporation to someone else. Hence, legal personhood is a status, whereas a legal platform is a construct. Untangling this systematic ambiguity will have some implications for the question of who or what can be a legal person, which will be addressed below.

Can Anything Be a Legal Person?

Following Naffine, one can roughly distinguish two approaches to the domain of legal personhood, that is, who or what can be a legal person. Legalism is typically accompanied by what I term the "Anything-Goes View", according to which anything – or almost anything – can be a legal person. Given the connection that realism posits between personhood and legal personhood, many realists likely do not accept the Anything-Goes Approach. However, as noted above, relying on the legalist/realist distinction can be somewhat misleading, given the number of positions packed within it. One way of understanding the monist/pluralist distinction is as a thesis about who or what *can* be legal persons. Here, we can distinguish the Only-Persons View from the Some-Limits View. According to the Only-Persons View – as the name implies – only persons can be legal persons. I endorse the Some-Limits view: I do not think that anything can be a legal person, but neither do I think that only persons could be legal persons.

I have elsewhere argued that the domain of legal personhood is mainly limited to sentient beings and group agents – with AI systems as a possible third case – but I do not intend to reproduce that argument here. Rather, I hope to provide an overview of what exactly the disagreement can be about.[66]

David J. Gunkel and Jordan Wales have in a recent paper endorsed the Anything-Goes View:

> If we ask the question, 'can AI be legal persons?' the answer is unequivocally 'yes,' but not because of what the AI is (or is not). It is because of the way law works. All that is necessary for something to be recognized as a legal person is for some legal authority – the head of state, a legislature, or a court of law – to decide that, for whatever reason, some specific AI has legal status as a person.[67]

---

[66] For some of my arguments, see Visa AJ Kurki, "Can Nature Hold Rights? It's Not as Easy as You Think" (2022) 11 Transnational Environmental Law 525; Kurki, *A Theory of Legal Personhood* (n 17) Chapter 4.

[67] David J Gunkel and Jordan Joseph Wales, "Debate: What Is Personhood in the Age of AI?" (2021) 36 AI & SOCIETY 473, 475. See also e.g. Michael Hartney, "Some Confusions

The authors do not here present an argument, but rather an assertion. However, the presented view is certainly alluring and even commonsensical: legislatures and other legal authorities may purport to confer legal personhood on any entity X if they choose to (assuming they are acting within any constitutional and other such doctrinal limits). Hence, any X can a legal person. However, legal scholars and theorists should not necessarily accept that all such acts are successful in actually endowing X with legal personhood. Rather, there may very well be limits on what entities can meaningfully be legal persons.

We can first consider some extreme cases. As I am writing this, I occasionally sip coffee. Can the sip that occurred on 26 June 2022 at 5.35pm be conferred legal personhood? A positive answer is highly implausible. It would be hard to understand what a legislative decision conferring legal personhood upon that sip would even mean. Once we – hopefully – agree that there are some limits to what entities are potential legal persons, the question remains what these limits are.[68] We can here distinguish disagreements around three types of questions: *conceptual, factual,* and *ethical.*[69]

The most important conceptual question here has to do with what the conferral of legal personhood to some X presupposes of X. I more or less agree with Neil MacCormick that a prerequisite for legal personhood are "capability to have interests and to suffer harm, and capability for rational and intentional action".[70] The capacity for rational action, however, is only required for active legal personhood, i.e. the kind of legal personhood that adults possess but infants do not. Ascribing legal personhood to an entity presupposes at least an ascription of interests to that entity: that things can be "good" or "bad" for that entity. A proponent of the Anything-Goes View might very well reject these kinds of conceptual limitations on entities. Rather, they might insist that an entity can be a legal person, in spite of having neither interests nor agency. One argument to this effect has to do with legal positivism: if we take legal positivism seriously, we must accept that the legislator can give legal personhood to whatever it wants. However, this view is confused. Though the legislator may – within constitutional limits – enact any kind of laws it chooses to, it is still up to legal scholars to provide explanations and analyses of said laws. For instance,

---

Concerning Collective Rights" (1991) 4 Canadian Journal of Law & Jurisprudence 293, 301–2; Richard Tur, "The 'Person' in Law" in Arthur Peacocke and Grant Gillett (eds), *Persons and Personality: A Contemporary Inquiry* (Basil Blackwell 1988).

[68] See also Paweł Banaś, "Why Cannot Anything Be a Legal Person?" (2021) Revus. Journal for Constitutional Theory and Philosophy of Law / Revija za ustavno teorijo in filozofijo prava 163–71. https://journals.openedition.org/revus/7335?lang=fr accessed 5 December 2022.

[69] By distinguishing "factual" from "ethical", I do not mean pick sides in metaethics. There might be ethical facts as well.

[70] MacCormick (n 23) 7. MacCormick talks about "the existence of a person", but I understand him to be addressing legal personhood.

the fact that corporations exist is clearly due to legal decisions. However, legal scholars may still provide various analyses of corporations: they may, for instance, argue that corporations do not "really" exist but are rather best understood as reducible to human individuals. Similarly, legal scholars may argue that laws treating, say, rivers as legal persons are valid, but best explainable as something else than that the river itself is a legal person. Now, perhaps it makes sense to say that rivers can be legal persons, but this is a matter of argumentation, rather than of fiat.[71]

As regards factual disagreement, non-Western ontologies – views of what there is in the world – are apparent in many cases involving rights of nature. Sources of law that ascribe rights to nature or ecosystems often recognise the traditional beliefs of certain indigenous peoples. For instance, according to Section 12 of the Te Awa Tupua (Whanganui River Claims Settlement) Act, "Te Awa Tupua is an indivisible and living whole, comprising the Whanganui River from the mountains to the sea, incorporating all its physical and metaphysical elements".[72] In Section 13, Te Awa Tupua is also described as "a spiritual and physical entity" and an "indivisible and living whole". Though these declarations can be given different interpretations, they can be seen as espousing a non-Western and non-secular ontology. Now, if one accepts such claims about the world, it will probably make sense to think of Te Awa Tupua as a legal person: it is likely endowed with interests, and perhaps with agency as well. However, if one instead opts for a Western, secular worldview, the conclusion that Te Awa Tupua can be a legal person is less obvious.[73]

However, one might accept the conceptual criteria just presented – or some other similar set of criteria – and regardless adhere to the Anything-Goes View. For instance, Raimo Siltala seems to think that a "will" can be construed to entities:

> [D]ivine objects, such as religious idols and the holy scriptures of religions (Quran, Bible, Torah), cannot speak for themselves, but they need a priest, a prophet, or other spokesman to express their alleged voice and will. Still, there is no inherent objection against establishing a legal spokesman or other similar arrangement for a sacred object of nature, whether it be a river, a rock, a sacred forest, or some other nature formation. All it takes is the founding of

---

[71] For a more developed argument, see Kurki, "Can Nature Hold Rights?" (n 66).

[72] Te Awa Tupua (Whanganui River Claims Settlement) Act 2017.

[73] Similarly, if one thinks that the Christian God exists, it may very well make sense to think of him as a potential legal person. However, if one does not believe in God, any legal statements treating God as a legal person can be seen as mistaken: they treat non-existent beings as if they existed. Since only existing beings – or, at least, beings that have existed or that will exist – can have interests, be harmed or perform acts, beings that have never existed cannot be legal persons.

a legal guardianship or spokesman for the entity concerned in the form of a priesthood or similar arrangement.[74]

I find this implausible. Again, the issue boils down to ontology. If the priests truly think the rock in question has a will that they can interpret, it makes sense for them and for their community to treat the rock as a legal person. Regardless, one may insist that the rock is not really a legal person: it is not the kind of entity that the priests think it is. The priests might think that the rock has a soul, but souls do not actually exist, which will affect how the arrangement should be understood. It may be useful to distinguish between two points of view here: doctrinal and analytic. From a doctrinal point of view, describing the duties of the priests may indeed require assuming – or at least imagining – that the rock has a soul and a will. However, from a system-independent, analytic point of view, one may analyse the arrangement as not conferring legal personhood to the rock.

Finally, the ethical question has to do with the value-laden nature of the offered criteria for legal personhood. Whether some entity can have interests or be harmed is partly an ethical issue. The more specific criterion that I have offered for being a potential passive legal person is the capacity to hold claim-rights. Here, I prefer the interest theory of (claim-)rights, and interest theorists typically set forth partly ethical criteria on who or what can hold rights.[75] Joseph Raz claims that nonhuman animals cannot hold rights because they are not of ultimate value, whereas Kramer thinks that animals can hold rights.[76] Their different viewpoints here depend on ethical disagreement, not factual. For instance, consider whether plants can be legal persons. Two people might share a non-animistic, scientific worldview – denying that plants have souls – and yet disagree on whether plants are the kinds of beings that can hold rights and be wronged.

Who or What Should Be a Legal Person?

Let us then briefly consider the question of who or what *should* be a legal person – or, at least, endowed with some incidents of legal personhood.[77]

---

[74] Raimo Siltala, "Earth, Wind, and Fire, and Other Dilemmas in a Theory of Legal Personhood – a Vindication of Legal Conventionalism" (2021) Revus. Journal for Constitutional Theory and Philosophy of Law / Revija za ustavno teorijo in filozofijo prava 137–46. https://journals.open edition.org/revus/6974 accessed 20 November 2022.

[75] E.g. Matthew H Kramer, "Rights without Trimmings" in Matthew H Kramer, NE Simmonds and Hillel Steiner (eds), *A Debate over Rights: Philosophical Enquiries* (Oxford University Press 1998); Kramer (n 27); Joseph Raz, "On the Nature of Rights" (1984) XCIll Mind 194.

[76] Raz (n 75); Kramer (n 75); Kramer (n 27).

[77] Benjamin Sachs makes the claim that proceeding in terms of the individual incidents is the only feasible way to approach the "should" question. Sachs (n 59) 116.

Once again, distinctions are needed. The term "should" expresses an ought that can be understood in at least two ways: morally and practically. The moral question is: what entities should morally be endowed with legal personhood (as a matter of, say, justice)? The practical question is: assuming some goal X, what entities should be endowed with legal personhood? Providing an exhaustive account of all of the various rationales that might support endowing some X with legal personhood is difficult. However, I will now make some high-level distinctions.

In his discussion of the legal personhood of AI systems, Simon Chesterman notes that granting legal personhood to an AI system can be based on intrinsic or instrumental reasons, even if he does not spell out what he means by these two categories of reasons.[78] I take that endowing an entity with legal personhood *for its own sake* – because it deserves or is otherwise entitled to legal personhood – is an intrinsic reason. Intrinsic reasons are most likely moral. Instrumental reasons, on the other hand, are all other types of reasons to endow an entity with (incidents of) legal personhood. For instance, corporate legal personhood may be justified by the putative positive economic or societal effects of treating corporations as separate legal persons.[79]

Further to the instrumental/intrinsic distinction, many other distinctions can be drawn. When discussing the legal personhood of nature and natural objects, I have also distinguished between *instrumental* – which, for the sake of clarity, I will here call *practical* – and *symbolic* rationales for Rights of Nature.[80] A practical rationale has to do with what practical effects Rights-of-Nature provisions may bring about: they may for instance solve some issues of standing that have plagued traditional approaches to environmental protection. The symbolic rationale has to do with the values embedded in or expressed by legal language. Designating a sacred river as a legal person may serve as a symbol of respect for the religious beliefs of a people.

---

[78] Simon Chesterman, "Artificial Intelligence and the Limits of Legal Personality" (2020) 69 International and Comparative Law Quarterly 819, 820. See also Novelli, Bongiovanni and Sartor's distinction between two possible approaches: what can be termed *reasons-monism* and *reasons-pluralism*. Under reasons-monism, there is only a single reason or rationale for conferring legal personhood, whereas under reasons-pluralism, there can be several. (The three scholars call these approaches simply "monism" and "pluralism", but I have reserved these terms for a different purpose, which is why I call them "reasons-monism" and "reasons-pluralism" here.) Novelli, Bongiovanni, and Sartor (n 14).

[79] Instrumental reasons may be moral, however. For instance, according to utilitarianism, one should maximise the overall utility, and this applies also to legal personhood arrangements. If conferring legal personhood upon some AI systems for instrumental reasons would lead to the best results overall, then such conferral would be morally required, according to utilitarianism.

[80] Kurki, "Can Nature Hold Rights?" (n 66) 528–30.

However, moral and practical reasons are not necessarily *legal* reasons. In other words, the fact that some entity should, morally, be treated as a legal person does not yet mean that judges are under a legal obligation to treat it as a legal person.

The "Should" Question in Law: Natural Law and Legal Positivism

From a legal point of view, how the "should" question is addressed depends greatly on what school of legal thought one supports: natural law or legal positivism.

Natural law is the minority approach. Its supporters typically emphasise that one cannot detach law as it *is* from how it morally *should be*.[81] John Finnis has presented a natural-law thesis about who or what should be a legal person. I will now quote at length his discussion of three US Supreme Court cases where the Court had essentially denied personhood under the US Constitution to black people and foetuses, whereas it had held that corporations are persons under the Constitution:

> These judges asserted, in each case, that the law's own theory of persons and legal personality – of who counts as a person – prevented those arguments about unjust and unlawful treatment from having any purchase in judicial reasoning. The court in *Dred Scott* was persuaded (or professed to be persuaded) by "the attitude of the founders" that black Africans can never be constitutionally made US citizens; the court in *Byrn* was professedly persuaded by Hans Kelsen – and the court in *Roe* professedly by the inapplicability to the unborn of some of the 14th Amendment's references to persons – that the unborn cannot be constitutional persons even though corporations are (by judicial fiat) despite the inapplicability to corporations of some of the 14th Amendment's references to persons. In each of these cases the court should have thought, like the Romans, that law is for the sake of persons. It should, therefore, have judged that, prior to all legislation and prior even to constitutional text, we and our courts ought to have a realistic and just account of what persons are and who are persons, and ought then to interpret legal and constitutional provisions so as to align them as far as possible with that just and realistic juridical, juristic, legal account and principle.[82]

---

[81] Natural law emphasises the interconnections of law and morality, whereas legal positivists emphasise that the most salient putative connections between law and morality are contingent rather than conceptually necessary.

[82] John Finnis, "The Priority of Persons" in *Intention and Identity: Collected Essays Volume II* (Oxford University Press 2011) 46.

Finnis here propounds a thesis that he takes to apply to all legal systems. He also seems to subscribe to a monist view, according to which persons – and perhaps *only* persons – should be legal persons.[83]

A somewhat similar account can also be discerned in the so-called Philosophers' Brief, written by a number of philosophers originally in support of a US lawsuit demanding legal personhood for two chimpanzees. In the brief, the authors argue for why (certain) animals should be viewed as persons, implying that such an argument would then have legal relevance. Hence, the brief seems to proceed from the assumption that if certain animals are indeed persons, then this fact constitutes a reason for endowing them with legal personhood.[84]

On the other hand, a legal positivist will likely treat legal arguments as system-contingent: the validity of claims such as "all persons should be legal persons" will depend on the legal system in question. Similar arguments as those presented by Finnis and in the Philosophers' Brief might still be relevant in some legal systems. A positivist could argue, for instance, that a legal system is committed to some moral principles which, correctly understood, would extend legal personhood to entities that are not currently recognised as legal persons. For instance, consider a legal system that has in its constitution committed to justice and equality but that has not recognised animals as legal persons. One might then present the argument that the principles of justice and equality, correctly understood, give the judiciary legal reasons to endow (some) animals with legal personhood. Relatedly, if the statute of some country simply makes reference to "persons", then philosophical arguments of the kind "X is a metaphysical person, therefore X should fall under the ambit of the provision" may very well be relevant. However, in general, a positivist approach tends to understand the question of who or what should be a legal person primarily as a question falling under morality, politics or other such fields.

Let us now look closer at how legal personhood may function in legal reasoning.

Legal Reasoning with Legal Personhood

One important issue here has to do with whether legal personhood is merely a *legal conclusion* or whether it can also function as a *legal reason*. Legal personhood can certainly function as a conclusion: for instance, on the Orthodox View, we can reach the conclusion that if X holds rights, then X is

---

[83] For another monist argument, see Joshua Jowitt, "Legal Rights for Animals: Aspiration or Logical Necessity?" (2020) 11 Journal of Human Rights and the Environment 173.

[84] Kristin Andrews, Gary Comstock, Crozier GKD, et al., *Chimpanzee Rights: The Philosophers' Brief* (Routledge 2018).

a legal person. However, can legal personhood function as an "inference ticket" – can we draw legal conclusions based on the fact some X is a legal person?[85]

Many doctrinal legal concepts do function as inference tickets. For instance, in many jurisdictions, if some house is legally designated as protected for its historical or architectural value, various legal consequences follow from this protection. Hence, judges and officials may draw conclusions such as: This house is legally protected. Therefore, it may not be torn down.

Whether the same is true of legal personhood depends on how we define legal personhood. The Capacity-for-Rights view does treat legal personhood as an inference ticket, though in a very limited sense: if some X is a legal person, then that X can hold rights or duties. However, most other definitions of legal personhood do not work this way. Rather, legal personhood is in most regards better understood as a conclusion of the relevant legal materials: once we know the legal situation of some X, we can deduce whether that X is a legal person. However, there are a number of ways in which legal personhood can potentially function as an inference ticket.

One important class of inference tickets is what may be called *doctrinal personhood categories*. These are categories that pack a specific bundle of legal personhood incidents. The most central such category is that of a natural person – a status acquired by human beings once they are born, and lost once they are legally considered dead. Once we know that some X is a natural person, we can make all sorts of legal inferences about that individual's legal situation: we can assume that they can acquire private-law rights and duties; that they have legal standing; and so on. The same goes for many types of corporate forms: once we know that some entity is, say, a limited liability company or a foundation, we can again draw all sorts of conclusions about their legal situation. However, such reasoning is often bound to be defeasible, meaning that it can be defeated.

Statutes and other legal materials can also make reference to legal personhood, often to determine the scope of the statute or some part of it.[86] However, when legal materials make reference to "persons", it is not always clear what kind of persons are intended. "Person" may here refer to at least human beings, moral/metaphysical persons, or to human beings.

---

[85] Thanks to Tomasz Zyglewicz for suggesting the phrase "inference ticket".

[86] For instance, the full name of the European Data Protection Regulation is "Regulation (EU) 2016/679 of the European Parliament and of the Council of 27 April 2016 on the protection of *natural persons* with regard to the processing of personal data and on the free movement of such data, and repealing Directive 95/46/EC" (emphasis added). The purpose of the regulation is thus to protect the data of natural persons.

For instance, take the Canadian case *R*. v. *Sharpe*, which was about the possession of child pornography.[87] The relevant legal provision provides a number of alternative definitions of child pornography, one of which is "a photographic, film, video or other visual representation [...] that shows a *person* who is or is depicted as being under the age of eighteen years and is engaged in or is depicted as engaged in explicit sexual activity".[88] The court asks whether this definition covers also "imaginary" persons, such as those depicted in cartoons, and concludes that it does.[89] Susanna Lindroos-Hovinheimo takes this example to strengthen her claim that there is no "unambiguous conception of legal personhood".[90] However, it is not at all obvious that *R*. v. *Sharpe* is about *legal* personhood. Rather, it is much more plausible that "person" here means simply "human being". For instance, let us suppose that someone draws a graphic novel depicting 15-year-old slaves in ancient Rome as engaged in explicit sexual activity. A criminal defence according to which they were depicting slaves – legal nonpersons – rather than persons, would likely not be successful. On the other hand, depictions of the sexual acts of 15-year-old extraterrestrials who meet the criteria of metaphysical and moral personhood – and are therefore "persons" in one sense of the word – are likely not covered by the statutory definition, either. Hence, understanding "person" as meaning simply "human being" is the most credible interpretation of the term.

Do All Legal Systems Have Legal Personhood?

After going through various conceptual distinctions regarding legal personhood, we may briefly discuss whether legal personhood is universal, that is, whether all legal systems must – as a matter of conceptual necessity – have legal personhood. Much will, again, depend on how we define "legal personhood".

The paradigmatic way of understanding legal personhood in Western legal systems has been the subject of a historical development that could have gone differently. Hence, it is implausible to think that all legal systems must have the same *theories* and *conceptualizations* of legal personhood as are prevalent in contemporary Western legal thought. However, a legal system could exhibit a normative structure approximating legal personhood even if it did not actually have the concept of a legal person. For example, an outsider observing some legal systems could note that some human beings are, in that legal system, treated as legal persons and others as slaves and as nonpersons, even if the officials of that legal system lacked this conceptual distinction. However, even then, whether *all*

---

[87] *R*. v. *Sharpe*, (2001) 1 S.C.R. 45, 2001 SCC 2.
[88] Criminal Code – R.S.C., 1985, c. C-46 (Section 163.1), emphasis added.
[89] *R*. v. *Sharpe*, (2001) 1 S.C.R. 45, 2001 SCC 2, paras 37 and 38.
[90] Lindroos-Hovinheimo (n 13) 30–2.

legal systems must exhibit the person/nonperson normative structure is a difficult question. I will remain agnostic here, but I will present some potential arguments.

First, the more formal one's view of legal personhood is, the more plausible a universalist claim becomes. For instance, it is likely that all legal systems contain norms that give to some entities normative positions that would be classified as rights under the interest theory and the will theory of rights. Hence, if legal personhood is defined formally as simply the holding of rights, then it may be the case that all legal systems must necessarily divide the universe into persons and nonpersons. On the other hand, there are possible arguments for the universality of legal personhood even under substantive conceptions. For instance, one could argue for something approximating H. L. A. Hart's idea of the minimum content of natural law[91]: all legal systems require beings that are protected, can enter into legally enforceable transactions, and so on, or the legal system in question will not last but will descend into chaos. However, I will remain agnostic on this point.

Conclusion

This section has addressed a number of theoretical and philosophical distinctions underlying legal personhood. Many of these have had to do with the connections of legal personhood to other types of personhood. The next two sections will focus on specific categories of legal personhood: Section 3 on natural and artificial persons, and Section 4 on animals, nature, and AI systems.

3 Natural and Artificial Persons

This section will address the two "classical" categories of legal persons: natural and artificial persons, meaning roughly the legal personhood of human individuals and human collectivities.[92]

Natural Personhood: The Legal Personhood of Human Beings

As has already been discussed, natural personhood is the legal personhood of human beings. In European languages, the cognate phrase is typically either "natural person" (e.g. *natürliche Person*) or "physical person" (e.g. *persona fisica*).

The phrase "natural person" can be misleading in at least three ways. First, especially if "natural person" is contrasted with "legal person", one may think that the term refers to non-legal personhood, for example metaphysical personhood. Second, the term may also suggest that natural personhood is

---

[91] HLA Hart, *The Concept of Law* (Clarendon Press 1994) 193–9.

[92] Single-person corporations, however, are examples of artificial persons that attach to human individuals rather than human collectivities.

somehow not dependent on legal decisions. For instance, Alexis Dyschkant writes that "[h]umans are called 'natural' persons because they are persons in virtue of being born, and not by legal decree".[93] This claim is problematic from a legal-positivist point of view. As Neil MacCormick notes, relying on the ideas of Hans Kelsen, "[t]he so-called 'natural person' is in its legal personhood necessarily as juristic as the so called 'juristic' [i.e. artificial] person".[94] Natural personhood can be taken away by legal decree, even if modern human rights law guarantees legal personhood to all born and sentient human beings. Third, "natural person" may also understandably be taken to refer to environmental personhood, which is central for the movement to extend legal personhood to nature or natural entities.

Not all natural persons have the exact same status. A central distinction here is between what I term *passive* and *active legal personhood*. Infants are passive legal persons, meaning that they are not treated as agents in the eyes of the law: they cannot by themselves alone make legally binding decisions nor are they held legally responsible. Adults deemed to be of sound mind, on the other hand, are active legal persons: they can decide about their affairs and be held legally responsible. This passive/active distinction is relatively well established, especially in civilian jurisdictions.[95]

Natural personhood starts at birth. Hence, foetuses are not natural persons, even though Western jurisdictions share the *nasciturus* rule, according to which unborn can retroactively be treated as legal persons for certain purposes if they are later born alive. If the father of a child passes away before the child is born, the child will inherit the father if later born alive. Some jurisdictions have extended, or sought to extend, other incidents of legal personhood to the unborn as well. For instance, so-called personhood amendments in the US would typically extend certain rights associated with legal personhood to unborn children, often beginning from the moment of conception.[96] Natural personhood ends at death, even if it may be contested whether all rights of some X cease to exist at X's death.[97]

---

[93] Alexis Dyschkant, "Legal Personhood: How We Are Getting It Wrong" (2015) University of Illinois Law Review 1231, 2078.

[94] Neil MacCormick, "Persons as Institutional Facts" in Ota Weinberger and Werner Krawietz (eds), *Reine Rechtslehre im Spiegel ihrer Fortsetzer und Kritiker* (Springer 1988) 371.

[95] Even though the distinction clearly exists in the common law as well, common-law legal scholars often do not seem to make the conceptual distinction as explicitly as civilian jurists.

[96] See e.g. John Seymour, *Childbirth and the Law* (Oxford University Press 2000) Chapter 8; Bonnie Steinbock, *Life before Birth: The Moral and Legal Status of Embryos and Fetuses* (2nd ed., Oxford University Press 2011). For an overview of the US debate, see the foetal personhood roundtable hosted by the Washington and Lee Law Review: "When Does Life Legally Begin? Legislative and Judicial Power in America's Abortion Debate" https://lawreview.wlulaw.wlu.edu/category/online/roundtables/fetal-personhood/ accessed 19 December 2022.

[97] See e.g. Kramer (n 27).

Under modern Western law, natural personhood cannot be taken away; doing so would contravene various human rights obligations. How the inter-connections of human rights and legal personhood can be understood depends on one's view of legal personhood. Under a formal view of legal personhood – especially the Capacity-for-Rights view – legal personhood is seen as something distinct from the various individual human rights, and the "right to legal personhood" can be understood as a separate right. This view is apparent in Article 6 of the Universal Declaration of Human Rights, accord-ing to which "[e]veryone has the right to recognition everywhere as a person before the law". On the other hand, under a substantive view of legal personhood, legal personhood can be identified as being secured by various human rights. For instance, under the Bundle Theory, the protection of one's life, liberty and bodily integrity is an incident of legal personhood. Hence, Article 3 of the Declaration – according to which "[e]veryone has the right to life, liberty and security of person" – addresses one incident of legal personhood. However, from slavery[98] to the civil death of prisoners[99], history knows of many cases where human beings have lost – or never been granted – at least some incidents of legal personhood.

As discussed earlier, natural personhood is not a single monolith, but has rather two central aspects: passive and active. Infants start out as purely passive legal persons, and gradually become increasingly active. I will now look more closely at two special cases, which I have elsewhere argued to be a special case to which legal theorists have not devoted much attention: the legal personhood of children and persons with (cognitive) disabilities. This will also allow for some distinctions on the active/passive scale.

Children as Legal Persons[100]

Adults who are deemed to be of sound mind are, in Western legal systems, fully active legal persons. Thus, they may normally dispose of their rights and duties, enter into contracts freely and so on. Furthermore, they are held fully respon-sible under tort law and criminal law, as well as under other types of responsi-bility. I call this type of fully active legal personhood *independent legal personhood*.

On the other hand, infants are, under prevalent Western law, what I term *purely passive legal persons*: they do not bear any legal responsibilities nor can

---

[98] Watson (n 1); Fede (n 1); Gamauf (n 1).

[99] Harry David Saunders, "Civil Death: A New Look at an Ancient Doctrine" (1970) 11 William and Mary Law Review 988.

[100] This section contains excerpts from Visa Kurki, "Active but Not Independent: The Legal Personhood of Children" (2021) 30 Griffith Law Review 395.

they exercise legal competences. This full passivity may run counter to how some scholars think of the matter. For instance, the German legal scholar Friederike Wapler starts a handbook chapter by simply asserting that "[c]hildren can have rights *and duties*, such as being party to a sales contract, or purchasing or inheriting property" (emphasis added).[101] Wapler then goes on to discuss the notion of children's rights critically but does not address the question of obligations further.

I take the idea that infants bear duties to be motivated by the following reasoning. First, ownership and contracts do typically entail duties. Owning a piece of property may, for instance, incur an annual property tax. The question is, then, whether infants can own property and be parties to contracts. Western jurisdictions employ two primary strategies here. First, a solution favoured by many common-law countries is to use the notion of a trust: a piece of property owned by a child is, formally, understood as being part of a trust, with the child as the beneficiary. Civil-law countries, on the other hand, generally lack the notion of a trust. In many civil-law countries, children are instead understood to own the property directly. However, they only have the right to "enjoy" the property, rather than the right to "exercise" or "administer" it. This arrangement relates to the abovementioned civil-law concept of legal capacity, which is often defined in terms of the capacity to hold private-law rights *and duties*. Wapler is clearly referring to this doctrinal construction.

Infants can own property and be parties to contracts, and these legal institutions do typically entail duties. Can infants therefore bear duties? Many civilian property lawyers would likely say that the duty is the infant's, even if the infant is not in practice expected to fulfil the obligation. The main problem with this explanation is obvious: the infant is not really the party who is expected to do anything. Rather, this task falls upon the infant's representative. Hence, the explanation relies on a problematic notion of a duty.

I have argued that this kind of a situation is best understood as a triangular situation, depicted in Figure 3. Let us assume that Lauri is represented by Maria, who acts as his guardian. We should now distinguish three elements: Lauri, Maria, and Lauri's legal platform, i.e. the legal rights and duties of Lauri. Given that Lauri is an infant and therefore a purely passive legal person, he cannot administer his legal platform: he cannot exercise his rights or fulfil his duties. Instead, Maria administers the legal platform, and such administration is done in Lauri's name. Lauri is, however, the beneficiary of the platform: if there are, say, property rights in the platform, it is Lauri who should benefit from them, and Maria has the

---

[101] *"Kinder können Rechte und Pflichten haben, etwa Partei eines Kaufvertrages sein, Eigentum erwerben oder erben"*. Friederike Wapler, "Kinderrechte" in Johannes Drerup (ed), *Handbuch Philosophie der Kindheit* (J B Metzler Verlag 2019) 121.

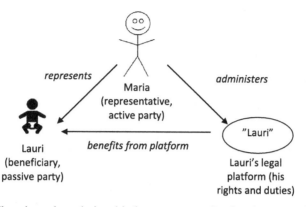

Figure 3 The triangular relationship between a passive legal person, their legal platform, and their representative

fiduciary duty to administer the legal platform. *There are* duties in Lauri's legal platform, which are currently borne by Maria. The bearer of these duties can change if Maria ceases to be Lauri's legal guardian. To reappropriate a metaphor of John Austin, Lauri can thus be understood as the 'compass' of the duty, who stays constant even if his representatives might change.[102] Lauri may also have several representatives who represent him in different capacities. For instance, Finnish law distinguishes between a child's custodians and guardians.[103] A more comprised way of expressing the same idea could be to label these duties as "proxy duties", signifying the idea that any talk of the "duties" of Lauri is really a shorthand for the duties of Lauri's proxy, whoever that proxy might be.

To sum up, neonates do not bear legal duties and should therefore not be understood as active legal persons. However, children leave full passivity at a relatively young age, as they gradually begin to be treated as legal actors. The treatment of children as active participants and agents – rather than merely as objects of protection – has increased significantly since the adoption of the Convention on the Rights of the Child in 1989.[104] Even relatively young children typically have some control over their rights and duties and can be held responsible to some extent. They are thus not fully passive, yet not independent either. This position can be labelled 'dependent active legal personhood', or *dependent legal personhood* for short.

This dependent legal personhood can take somewhat different forms. The "first stage" of dependent legal personhood is the right to be heard, which is held

---

[102] See John Austin, *Lectures on Jurisprudence: Or, the Philosophy of Positive Law, Vol. I* (John Murray, Albemarle Street 1885) 874.

[103] See Guardianship Services Act (*Holhoustoimilaki*, 442/1999).

[104] United Nations Convention on the Rights of the Child 1989, UN Doc A/44/25. The Convention entered into force in 1990.

Table 4 Three types of competences

Negative competences	The child can prevent a legal change, thus protecting the status quo.
Dependent competences	The child can effect a legal change, subject to the approval, veto or cancellation of, for example, her parent/guardian.
Independent competences	The child can effect a legal change independently.

already by young children according to the Convention on the Rights of Child. However, the right to be heard does not mean that one's views determine the outcome; rather, under the convention, the views of the child shall be given "due weight". A legal competence, on the other hand, is the capacity to effect an intentional legal change. Legal competences are thus determinative and conclusive. The child gains access to an incident of active legal personhood *par excellence* when she is endowed with her first competences.

As regards the legal competences of children, we can distinguish three main categories (see Table 4). First, a *negative* competence is the power to prevent a legal change, initiated by another. Second, *dependent* competences are subject to a consent, veto or cancellation by some other party. Finally, a competence is *independent* if its holder may freely decide to exercise it, and the legal effect is not subject to, for example, a consent by some other party.[105]

I will use the Finnish Act on the Freedom of Religion as an example because it contains an interesting provision that exemplifies these different categories.[106] As regards membership in a religious community, Section 3(1–3) sets out the following rules:

> Section 3
> Membership of a religious community
> Everyone has the right to decide on his or her religious affiliation by joining a religious community that accepts him or her as a member or by resigning from one.
> The decision on the religious affiliation of a child is made jointly by the persons who have custody of the child. [...]
> A child who has attained the age of 15 years may, however, personally join a religious community or resign from one with the written consent of the persons who have custody of the child. A person who has attained the age of

---

[105] Even dependent competences do of course have the immediate legal effect of enabling, say, the guardian to prevent the change.

[106] *Uskonnonvapauslaki* (453/2003).

12 years may be joined to a religious community or be notified as having resigned from one only with his or her written consent.

The provision thus contains four different categories:

(1) Children under 12 years old, whose religious affiliation is decided by those who have custody of them.

(2) Children between 12 and 17 years, who must consent to a change in their religious affiliation (*negative competence*, approval).

(3) Children between 15 and 17 years, who may initiate a change in their religious affiliation, though requiring the consent of their guardians (*dependent competence*).

(4) Adults, who may freely decide over their religious affiliation (*independent competence*).

The path of a child from a purely passive legal person to an independent legal person is thus a gradual development. Infants are not entitled to being heard nor are they endowed with legal competences. As the child grows older, she must be heard in an increasing number of contexts, and she will gradually also receive an increasing number of competences. Figure 4 depicts how law's relationship towards the child gradually shifts from paternalism to recognising the child's autonomy and independence.

Persons with Cognitive Disabilities

Persons with cognitive disabilities have traditionally been denied the competence to decide about their own affairs.[107] They have often been unable consent to medical procedures or even to sex.[108] However, in the recent years, disability law has seen

Figure 4 The competences that have been conferred to a child can be seen as an expression of the extent to which the legal system recognises the child's autonomy and independence, as opposed to taking a paternalistic stance towards the child

---

[107] For a more in-depth discussion of some the issues presented here, see Visa Kurki, "Expanding Agency and Borders of Competence" in Gonzalo Villa Rosas and Torben Spaak (eds), *Legal Power and Legal Competence: Meaning, Normativity, Officials and Theories* (Springer 2023).

[108] On the last point, see Anna Arstein-Kerslake, "Understanding Sex: The Right to Legal Capacity to Consent to Sex" (2015) 30 Disability and Society 1459.

a somewhat similar paradigm shift as the legal status of children. The agency, autonomy, and self-determination of persons with disabilities is increasingly emphasised, with the Convention on the Rights of Persons with Disabilities spearheading a new approach. Article 12 of the Convention includes the following sections:

(1) States Parties reaffirm that persons with disabilities have the right to recognition everywhere as persons before the law.

(2) States Parties shall recognise that persons with disabilities enjoy legal capacity on an equal basis with others in all aspects of life.

(3) States Parties shall take appropriate measures to provide access by persons with disabilities to the support they may require in exercising their legal capacity.

As noted in Section 1, the terminology here is ambiguous. The phrase "legal capacity" is often understood as the capacity to hold rights and duties. However, "legal capacity" in the Convention denotes instead the capacity to administer one's own legal situation through legal competences.[109] To make matters even more complicated, the phrase is also used to refer to both passive and active legal personhood.[110] In what follows, I take "legal capacity" to refer to active legal personhood, and in particular to legal competences.

The new approach spearheaded by the Convention, labelled "universal legal capacity", entails in particular that

> States must recognise universal legal capacity for all persons with disabilities, including for those requiring more intensive support. That entails adopting legislation that explicitly recognizes the capacity of persons with disabilities to create, modify or end legal relationships, as well as providing effective legal protection against any interference with such capacity. That recognition must include the exercise of the right to property, access to all forms of financial credit and the right to control one's own financial affairs.[111]

This is not to say that persons with disabilities need to make such decisions alone; rather, the individual should receive assistance, such as a circle of support consisting of people who are familiar with the individual. However, the

---

[109] The other central incident of active legal personhood has to do with bearing legal duties and being held responsible in criminal and tort law.

[110] For instance, a report by the Council of Europe Commissioner for Human Rights defines the phrase as follows: "Legal capacity can be described as a person's power or possibility to act within the framework of the legal system. In other words, it makes a human being a subject of law. It is a legal concept, a construct, assigned to most people of majority age enabling them to have rights and obligations, to make binding decisions and have them respected". Nilsson (n 22) 9–10. See also Dhanda (n 22), 442–3.

[111] Catalina Devandas Aguilar, "Universal Legal Capacity to Ensure the Equal Recognition of Persons with Disabilities before the Law (Report of the Special Rapporteur on the Rights of Persons with Disabilities A/HRC/37/56)" (UN Human Rights Council 2017) 19.

individual may at any time reject the support. This arrangement is denoted *supported decision-making.*

On the other hand, "regimes of substituted decision-making" must be abolished. Under such regimes, "legal capacity is removed from a person (even if limited to a single decision) and a substitute decision maker appointed by a third party takes decisions based on what he or she considers is in the best interests of the person concerned, even if that goes against the will of the latter".[112] The Convention thus gives precedence to the will, rather than the best interests, of individuals with disabilities.

In conclusion, the new regime introduced by the Convention requires treating persons with disabilities increasingly as active legal persons.

Artificial Personhood: The Legal Personhood of Collectivities

The prime example of artificial persons is the corporation. In fact, the term "corporation" may even be understood as more or less synonymously with "artificial person"; this depends on some ambiguities pertaining to "corporation".

First, in predominantly American usage, "corporation" refers to business corporations – and often specifically the limited liability company.[113] According to a broader, typically UK usage, "corporation" also includes other incorporated entities, such as universities, nonprofits, and so on. For instance, the University of Oxford describes itself as a "civil corporation".[114] In what follows, I will use "corporation" in the broader sense. However, it is often difficult to keep the two senses completely distinct. For instance, scholars who purport to address corporations in the broader sense often regardless use limited-liability companies as their primary example, which may very well affect the overall analysis.

The second ambiguity is of a theoretical nature. As I've noted in Section 1 when introducing the person/platform and the status/construct distinctions, discussions of legal personhood – and corporations in particular – often oscillate between two ways of understanding a corporation. The corporation can be understood as an entity – such as an organised group of scholars or entrepreneurs – that has a particular, incorporated legal status, but it can also be understood as a construct: as a bundle of rights and duties. I will return to this distinction below.

A third ambiguity with the discussion of corporate personhood has to do with the fact that especially in the US discourse, there is not always a clear distinction

---

[112] Aguilar (n 111) 7.

[113] In this narrow sense of "corporation", commercial partnerships may be classified as legal persons and yet not as corporations.

[114] www.ox.ac.uk/about/organisation/university-as-a-charity, visited on 25 November 2022.

between the *constitutional* personhood[115] of business corporations – a doctrine mostly limited to the US – as opposed the more general phenomenon that corporations are legal persons. For instance, in European human rights doctrine, business corporations are typically not treated as holders of human or constitutional rights.[116] Regardless, business corporations are legal persons in Europe.

A Very Brief History of Corporations

To understand corporations, we should briefly consider their history in Western law. I will now briefly discuss the history of corporations in general as well as the origins of modern business corporations and of the US doctrine treating corporations as constitutional persons.

The notion of a corporation – in the broad sense of the term – dates back to Roman law. The first Roman corporations (*universitates*, singular *universitas*) were public bodies such as cities and states. They could own property and enter into contracts in their own name. It has been suggested that the notion of a corporation spread throughout Europe with the Roman administration.[117] In the Middle Ages, the notion of monasteries' owning property was important, as for instance monks were not allowed to own property. As a result, the canon-law status of monasteries and other corporations needed to be specified. Famously, Pope Innocent IV declared them to be fictional persons (*personae ficta*). Some norms applying to human beings, such as the possibility of excommunication, did not apply to fictional persons, but they could regardless have their own assets.[118]

The earliest examples of modern business corporations were the English East India Company and the Dutch East India Company, founded in 1600 and 1602, respectively. These companies exhibited at least one feature of modern business corporations: they were joint-stock companies. However, it is disputed whether these companies already exhibited the second crucial feature of modern business corporations: the limited liability of shareholders. Some scholars argue that they did, whereas others place the emergence of limited liability at the 1850s or even as late as the 1930s.[119]

---

[115] In my preferred terminology, "subjecthood". See the discussion on Legal subjecthood in Section 1.

[116] For one comparison, see Ioana Cismas and Stacy Cammarano, "Whose Right and Who's Right: The US Supreme Court v. the European Court of Human Rights on Corporate Exercise of Religion" (2016) 34 Boston University International Law Journal 1.

[117] William L Burdick, *The Principles of Roman Law and Their Relation to Modern Law* (The Lawbook Exchange 2004) 281–7.

[118] John Dewey, "The Historic Background of Corporate Legal Personality" (1926) 35 Yale Law Journal 655, 664–5.

[119] For an overview as well as an argument for the last option, see Ron Harris, "A New Understanding of the History of Limited Liability: An Invitation for Theoretical Reframing" (2020) 16 Journal of Institutional Economics 643. The UK case *Salomon v. Salomon* is

The emergence of the US doctrine of the constitutional personhood of business corporations is usually traced back to how the US Supreme Court interpreted the Equal Protection Clause of the 14th Amendment, which states that no state shall "deny to any person within its jurisdiction the equal protection of the laws". In the 1880s, the Court declared that corporations are "persons" within the ambit of said clause.[120] The implications of the constitutional personhood of corporations have been subject to a considerable body of case law; one of the most famous recent cases is *Citizens United*, which declared restrictions on election campaign spending by incorporated entities as unconstitutional on the grounds that they violated the free speech of corporations.[121]

Theories of Corporations

A scholarly discussion of corporations typically proceeds from a relatively canonical list of so-called corporate theories. Often, at least three kinds of theories are listed: the *association* (or *aggregate* or *partnership*) theory, the *grant* (or *concession* or *fiction*) theory and the *real-entity* theory.[122] The association theories explain corporations in a "bottom-up" manner: companies consist of individuals coming together, and the interests of corporations are, actually, the interests of said individuals. Grant theories explain corporations as creations of the law. Finally, real-entity theories typically emphasise the "pre-existing" nature of corporations: they are collectives that "really" exist, and the law simply provides recognition of this fact.[123]

However, one should be careful here. First, it is not always obvious whether these theories are mainly offered as theories of business corporations or rather of incorporated entities more broadly. Second, merely listing different corporate theories – often presented, at least implicitly, as mutually exclusive alternatives – can even be misleading. For instance, David Millon analyses corporate theories in terms of three dimensions:

---

sometimes presented as crucial for corporate legal personhood more generally, but it mainly affirmed the doctrine of the limited liability of shareholders. *Salomon* v. *A Salomon & Co Ltd* [1897] AC 22.

[120] The most important cases in this regard are *Santa Clara County* v. *Southern Pacific Railroad*, 118 U. S. 394, and *Minneapolis & St. Louis Ry. Co.* v. *Beckwith*, 129 U.S. 26 (1889).

[121] *Citizens United* v. *Federal Election Commission*, 558 U.S. 310 (2010).

[122] Paul Kens, "Nothing to Do with Personhood: Corporate Constitutional Rights and the Principle of Confiscation" (2015) 34 Quinnipiac Law Review 1. In his recent overview, Joshua Gellers for some reason distinguishes the real-entity theory (which he labels the "unique entity theory") from what he labels the "reality theory". Gellers (n 29) 33. I take the real-entity theory and the reality theory to fall under the same category.

[123] Eric W Orts, *Business Persons: A Legal Theory of the Firm* (Oxford University Press 2013) 9–26.

(1) *entity/aggregate:* "the corporation as an entity, with a real existence separate from its shareholders and other participants, and the corporation as a mere aggregation of natural individuals without a separate existence";

(2) *artificial/natural:* "the corporation as an artificial creation of state law and the corporation as a natural product of private enterprise"; and

(3) *public/private:* corporations have "broad social and political ramifications that justify a body of corporate law that is deliberately responsive to public interest concerns", as opposed to "corporate law as governing little more than the private relations between the shareholders of the corporation and management, which acts as their agents".[124]

We can see here that, for instance, the real-entity and aggregate theories will differ on the first axis, but they may very well agree on the second axis: both will likely see the (business) corporation as arising out private enterprise.

Different theories may also seek to explain different aspects of corporations. Petri Mäntysaari distinguishes between legal and economic theories of corporations.[125] The abovementioned theories are typically legal theories, and more specifically *doctrinal* theories: they often seek to explain what rights and duties corporations have, or should have, as a matter of the law of some jurisdiction. Hence, for instance, grant theories emphasise that corporations have only those rights and duties that have been explicitly granted to them. Some theorists have also emphasised that limited liability is a type of "privilege" granted to limited liability companies – a privilege that also justifies additional duties imposed upon such companies.[126] Associate theories, on the other hand, may quite naturally favour a broader set of rights and/or duties, because the rights of corporations are an extension of the rights of the participants.[127] On the other hand, *philosophical* theories of corporations – recently often propounded as part of the emerging field of social ontology – typically seek to provide an analytical and descriptive explanation of corporations. I will now briefly discuss two issues

---

[124] David Millon, "Theories of the Corporation" (1990) 1990 Duke Law Journal 201–2.

[125] Petri Mäntysaari, *Organising the Firm: Theories of Commercial Law, Corporate Governance and Corporate Law* (Springer-Verlag 2012) 57–74.

[126] Lyman Johnson remarks that in 2012, "the editors of the market-favoring publication the Economist noted that 'limited liability is a privilege' and 'a concession – something granted by society because it has a clear purpose'". Lyman Johnson, "Law and Legal Theory in the History of Corporate Responsibility: Corporate Personhood Berle III: Theory of the Firm: The Third Annual Symposium of the Adolf A. Berle, Jr. Center on Corporations, Law & Society" (2011) 35 Seattle University Law Review 1135, 1149f. (citing Corporate Anonymity–Light and Wrong, *The Economist*, 21 January 2012, at 16, available at www.economist.com/node/21543164).

[127] This is what I take the US politician Mitt Romney to have meant with his infamous statement "Corporations are people, my friend": corporations are, really, the people behind the corporations.

from this analytical point of view: the social-ontological nature of corporations, and the nature of the legal act of incorporation.

Analytical Questions

When addressing what corporations *are* – rather than, for example, what legal rights they *should have* – I take the most appropriate labels for the alternatives to be *realism* and *fictionalism*.

A realist approach takes collectivities to "really" exist, independent of their legal status: they are, for instance, conceived of as group agents, meaning organised groups that – as a result of the organisation – exhibit agency that is clearly distinct from the agency of the individual members. What incorporation means, then, is giving these collectivities a specific legal status. I have elsewhere used the metaphor of a "visibility cloak": incorporation renders group agents visible within the law, enabling them, for instance, to perform legally enforceable transactions.[128]

A fictionalist approach, on the other hand, provides a different descriptive account of the corporation. According to this approach, corporations are examples of the kinds of imaginary constructs that law can create: corporations exist "only in contemplation of law", as the US Supreme Court has put it.[129] Fictionalism can in fact take two rather different forms, having to do with the ambiguity of the term "fiction". In the narrower "as-if" sense, "fiction" refers to the law pretending that something is the case.[130] A classic example of a fiction theory in the "as-if" sense is the theory of Friedrich Carl von Savigny. According to Savigny, only human beings are "real" persons because they have the kind of inner freedom that is requisite of persons.[131] The idea of a corporation, therefore, has to do with creating an artificial person and thereby treating non-persons as persons for legal purposes.[132] We can see that Savigny is here positing a connection between personhood and legal personhood, and thereby assuming a monist position about legal personhood (see Section 2).

In a broad sense, "fiction" means simply "social fact". A social fact is, roughly put, a fact that depends on the beliefs and attitudes of some social group. For instance, the existence of money is a social fact: whether some piece

---

[128] Kurki, *A Theory of Legal Personhood* (n 17) 167.

[129] *Trustees of Dartmouth College* v. *Woodward*, 17 US 518 (1819) 636.

[130] See H Vaihinger, *The Philosophy of "As If", A System of the Theoretical, Practical and Religious Fictions of Mankind* (2nd ed., Kegan Paul, Trench, Trubner 2006).

[131] Savigny was also a will theorist of rights, so possessing an autonomous will was, on his account, central for the capacity to hold rights.

[132] See Friedrich Carl von Savigny, *System des heutigen römischen Rechts* (Veit 1840) book 2, § 85.

of fabric is money depends on whether we collectively treat it as such.[133] In this broad sense, corporations are almost indisputably fictions: corporations' existence depends on various beliefs and attitudes of human beings.

However, some scholars emphasise how corporations can be created "out of thin air". For instance, John Searle argues that when a new corporation is formed, nothing *becomes* a corporation:

> In this case we seem to have created a remarkably potent object, a limited liability corporation, so to speak out of thin air. No preexisting object was operated on to turn it into a corporation.[134]

For Searle, a corporation is "free-standing", meaning that nothing *counts* as a corporation. Hence, corporations are not pre-existing entities – such as group agents – that are given a legal status, but rather simply legal creations. In the terminology introduced in Section 2, corporations are constructs rather than statuses.

I believe that the Searlean and the realist pictures can be combined. As noted above, the word "corporation" is occasionally used to refer to an entity with a legal status, and occasionally to the *status* (or *construct*) *itself* – to a bundle of rights and duties. In this latter sense, there is nothing that is made into a legal person; a new "legal person" simply comes into being. This sense of legal-person-*qua*-legal-positions becomes most apparent when we consider so-called single-person corporations, possible in some jurisdictions.

Let us say that Mary starts a veterinary practice. She wants to keep her business-related assets and liabilities separate from her private assets and liabilities, so she starts a one-person corporation, Mary Inc., for her business. She now has two personas, "legal masks", through which to sign contracts, own property and so on: "Mary" and "Mary Inc.". These two masks are just two bundles of legal positions (rights and duties), both attaching to Mary. Corporations *qua* bundles of rights and duties may be called *corporate platforms*,[135] whereas a group agent with the legal status of a corporation may be denoted an *incorporated collectivity*.

Exposing this ambiguity about corporations can also serve towards clarifying certain puzzles in social ontology. For instance, let us reconsider Searle's position. According to Searle, a corporation is "free-standing", meaning that

---

[133] See Searle (n 62).

[134] Searle (n 16) 98. Note that for Searle, everything still bottoms out in the physical world.

[135] We should be careful not to reify things unnecessarily here. I talked of "entities" above, and corporations are often referred to as legal entities. The term "entity" may mean various things, but I would argue that the corporate platform is reducible to a bundle of legal positions. There is no entity over and above these positions; all relevant features of corporate platforms are explainable in terms of the rights and duties and their interactions.

nothing *counts* as a corporation. Clues such as Searle's characterisation of the corporation as "power relationships between actual people" suggest that he seems to be thinking of corporations as corporate platforms.[136] Many critics of Searle have disputed this understanding of corporations. Frank Hindriks argues instead that organisations such as corporations are "constituted by one or more persons"[137], and that "the members count as an organisation with a particular status".[138] Hindriks, thus, understands corporations as incorporated collectivities. The two can therefore be said to be using the term in different senses.

"Corporation" can thus refer both to corporate platforms and to incorporated collectivities. Some disagreements in corporate theory can potentially be understood in terms of differing explananda: theories that treat corporations as mere legal creations seek to explain corporations *qua* legal platforms, whereas theories that accord corporations a more robust status understand them as group agents with a specific legal status.

To wrap up our discussion of artificial persons, we can note that even seemingly incompatible theories may coexist to some extent. For instance, consider theories seeking to explain the ontology of corporations at a general level *vis-à-vis* theories addressing the constitutional status of corporations. One might hold that corporations really exist as collectives, and regardless think that merely this fact does not entitle them to any constitutional rights. Instead, one might employ the association theory to assess whether corporations should be treated as holders of some constitutional rights: essentially, any constitutional rights of corporations should be justified by the constitutional rights of their shareholders.

New Configurations of Legal Personhood: Natural or Artificial?

This section has addressed the "classical" categories of legal personhood: natural and artificial personhood. I will conclude by briefly addressing how these two categories relate to the potential new categories of legal personhood.

Traditionally, the difference between natural and artificial persons has been relatively clear: natural persons are born human individuals, whereas artificial persons are all other types of legal persons. However, given new the potential

---

[136] Searle writes: "Notice also that the whole point of doing this is to create a rather elaborate set of power relationships between actual people; indeed, the corporation consists of such relationships". Searle (n 16) 98.

[137] Frank Hindriks, "But Where Is the University?" (2012) 66 Dialectica 93, 105.

[138] ibid 106. For a more legal-oriented discussion of the interactions of social ontology and corporate theory, see Eric W Orts, "Theorizing the Firm: Organizational Ontology in the Supreme Court" (2016) 65 DePaul Law Review 559.

and realised categories of legal personhood, one may ask what exactly constitutes the difference between these two categories. Would, say, animal legal persons be classified under natural or artificial personhood, or would they constitute a new category? The answer is not obvious. For instance, there are at least two plausible ways to understand the category of natural personhood.

First, natural personhood can be understood in terms of how the concept is labelled in many Romance languages: as the legal personhood of physical beings (*personnes physiques, personas físicas*).[139] Hence, the legal personhood of animals would be a subtype of natural personhood because it concerns individual animals, who are legal persons from birth to death and whose legal platform is fixed, that is, non-transferrable between different entities.[140] For instance, in their proposed taxonomy of the legal personhood of animals, Caroline Regad and Cedric Riot categorise animals under natural personhood.[141]

On the other hand, natural personhood can be understood as being reserved for human beings merely, whereby nonhuman animals endowed with legal personhood should not be classified as natural persons. This option would at least have the benefit that "natural person" is a phrase used in statutes, normally with the intention to refer to human beings. Not classifying animals as natural persons would not upset how such phrases are to be interpreted. Instead, animals could be classified under artificial persons, or a third category could be introduced. Classifying animals as artificial persons is a somewhat awkward option. A typical feature of artificial persons is that the associated physical entities can change. For instance, the owners and staff of a business corporation may be completely replaced over time. Hence, the category of artificial persons would become rather heterogeneous if animals were classified as such; introducing a completely new category might therefore be preferable.

The next, and final, section of this Element will focus on these emerging categories of legal personhood: animals, nature, and AI systems.

---

[139] There are some special cases where this way of demarcating between natural and artificial persons does not hold. For instance, Shawn Bayern has argued that artificial intelligence systems could be given legal personhood by employing the highly flexible corporate law of the US: the AI system could be given complete and irrevocable control over the corporation. In this case, one might argue that the putative artificial personhood has transformed into a form of natural personhood for the AI system ''Shawn Bayern, 'The Implications of Modern Business-Entity Law for the Regulation of Autonomous Systems' (2015) 19 Stanford Technology Law Review 93.

[140] Barring special cases, e.g. X assuming the identity of Y.

[141] Caroline Regad, "Les animaux liés à un fonds, vers une nouvelle categorie de personnes physiques non-humaines" in Caroline Regad and Cédric Riot (eds), *La personnalité juridique de l'animal (II): Les animaux liés à un fonds (les animaux de rente, de divertissement, d'expérimentation)* (LexisNexis 2020).

4 Emerging Categories of Legal Personhood: Animals, Nature, and AI

This section will address the recent discussion and case law surrounding three cases of the (potential) extension of legal personhood to nonhumans: animals, the nature – including parts of the nature, such as natural areas – and AI systems.

Before moving on to discuss the three topics just outlined, it is worth briefly considering the rationales behind giving legal personhood and/or rights to these entities. Simon Chesterman's distinction between intrinsic and instrumental reasons, discussed in Section 2, may again serve as a useful starting point. As noted earlier, a reason to endow some entity X with legal personhood *for X's own sake* – because it deserves or is otherwise entitled to legal personhood – is an intrinsic reason. Instrumental reasons, on the other hand, are all other types of reasons to endow X with (incidents of) legal personhood.

Arguments for the legal personhood of animals, nature and AI systems may all be based on either intrinsic or instrumental reasons. In the case of animals, arguments based on intrinsic reasons are clearly more prevalent: typically, arguments for the legal personhood of animals are based on, for example, their interests, moral rights, moral personhood or other such reasons. However, instrumental reasons may also be invoked here. For instance, many point to how current practices of animal exploitation are connected to problems facing humanity as well: practices such as factory farming contribute to climate change, ecosystem degradation, zoonoses, and so on. Hence, given that the legal personhood of animals would arguably reduce such practices, there are instrumental reasons for animal legal personhood. Pet trusts – a way for human beings to give property to their companion animals – can also be understood as being based on instrumental reasoning: rather than being based on animals' interests, the existence of said trusts is primarily motivated by concern for human beings' connection with certain individual animals.

Both individual and intrinsic reasons are also apparent in the case of Rights of Nature and AI legal personhood. For instance, Rights of Nature and environmental personhood can be seen as motivated by the ultimate value of nature or some natural entities, but it can also be seen as a tool for preserving some natural entities for future human generations. In the legal literature, discussions of the legal personhood of AI systems are often motivated by instrumental reasoning. These discussions often make reference to accountability gaps, economic efficiency and other such reasons that do not justify the AI system's legal personhood with its interests, moral rights, well-being or other such reason. However, philosophers have also showed ample interest in the intrinsic side as well.[142]

---

[142] See David J Gunkel, "The Other Question: Can and Should Robots Have Rights?" (2017) Ethics and Information Technology 1.

I will now discuss animals, nature, and AI in turn.

Animal Legal Personhood

The Finnish legal scholar Wilhelm Lavonius offered already in the 1860s an argument for the legal personhood of animals. He wrote:

> The animal has a sense of its existence, feels itself and [...] to some extent the surrounding world [...]. Each animal has its own essence, its own determination [...]. The animal is therefore not solely an object of rights, but, on the contrary, should be regarded as a legal subject, an entity that has rights.[143]

Lavonius was in a minority during his time, but the calls for animal rights and legal personhood have increased during the late twentieth and, especially, the twenty-first century.

The animal rights movement demands, roughly put, the better treatment of animals. In its mainstream form, the movement emphasises the similarities between human beings and (some) other animals, arguing that animals, too, possess some of the features that establish moral considerability for humans. A legal application of animal ethics is the Nonhuman Rights Project, which seeks to have certain animals declared as legal persons and as holders of legal rights, typically for the purposes of *habeas corpus*, the writ protecting the right to personal freedom.[144] This kind of animal ethics is typically individualistic, in that its primary concern is individual animals, rather than, for example, the survival of species or biodiversity.

I will now first discuss how the current legal status of animals can be understood, and what exactly would be needed to change their status to that of right-holders and/or legal persons. I will then briefly discuss proposals for how the legal status of animals *should* look like.

Animal Status de lege lata

There is, in fact, considerable disagreement on the current state of affairs: whether animals already are legal persons and/or right-holders, and what exactly would be needed to turn them into such.

We can again distinguish a formal and a substantive approach to the legal status of animals. The binary, formal view – often based on the Orthodox View of legal personhood (and, more broadly, the Orthodox Inventory) – understands animals currently as (1) property, (2) nonpersons, and (3) without rights.

---

[143] Wilhelm Lavonius, *Vuosikertomus Eläintensuojelus-Yhdistyksen Helsingissä yleiseen kokoukseen* (Eläintensuojelus-Yhdistys Helsingissä 1876) 3.

[144] See www.nonhumanrights.org/ (visited on 1 December 2022).

Furthermore, on this view, turning animals into legal persons would typically require some kind of an explicit, formal act, such as a declaration by a court or a legislature stating that animals are legal persons or that they have rights. On the other hand, a substantive view offers a different way of approaching the matter. On a substantive view, animals could already hold legal rights while remaining as property, and their legal status could gradually shift towards legal personhood.

Discussions of animal legal personhood have mostly been dominated by the formal Orthodox View. Most theoretically-oriented animal law scholars have assumed that, in typical Western jurisdictions, animals are neither legal persons nor holders of legal rights. One influential legal-theoretical view has been that of Steven Wise, who has in his works assumed that animals must first be declared legal persons, with the capacity to hold rights, before they can actually hold rights.[145] His view thus falls under what I call the Capacity-for-Rights view, a version of the Orthodox View. The Capacity-for-Rights view still structures jurists' thinking about animal rights; it is likely especially powerful among civil lawyers, who are in their legal studies often taught the Capacity-for-Rights view as the definition of legal personhood.

However, not all scholars and judges follow the approach just outlined. First, some have argued that animals, in fact, already hold rights. For instance, Cass Sunstein and the federal judge in the *Tilikum* case have both stated that animals already have rights as a result of animal welfare laws.[146] I myself have put forward a similar argument, as have for example Clare McCausland and Alasdair Cochrane.[147] Saskia Stucki has presented the useful distinction between simple rights and fundamental rights. According to Stucki, animals could be said to hold simple rights as a result of animal welfare laws, but not fundamental rights, meaning strong, broad and properly enforceable rights.[148]

Another interesting example of animals' potentially already holding rights is the issue of pet trusts. Some US states already allow for pet owners to leave some money in a trust, with their companion animal as the beneficiary. Given that such arrangements are typically understood as ownership, one may in fact argue that companion animals can already own property. Hence, such pets have, in fact, already been endowed with at least one incident of legal

---

[145] See for instance. Steven M Wise, *Rattling the Cage: Toward Legal Rights for Animals* (Perseus 2000).

[146] *Tilikum et al. v. Sea World Parks & Entertainment Inc.*, 842 F. Supp. 2d 1259 (S.D. Cal. 2012) and Cass Sunstein, "Can Animals Sue?" in Cass R Sunstein and Martha C Nussbaum (eds), *Animal Rights: Current Debates and New Directions* (Oxford University Press 2004).

[147] McCausland (n 36); Alasdair Cochrane, "Do Animals Have an Interest in Liberty?" (2009) 57 *Political Studies* 660.

[148] Stucki (n 27).

personhood – and a significant incident at that.[149] However, though such arrangements constitute a rather significant departure from how animals have traditionally been placed in the person/thing dichotomy, these arrangements can also be seen as problematic from an ethical point of view, given that they prioritise certain animals that humans have bonded with, rather than giving rights to animals on an equal basis.[150]

Scholars departing from the formal paradigm have also outlined alternative ways towards animal legal personhood than the path of formal declaration. Eva Bernet Kempers has argued that the potential progress of animals towards legal personhood could also happen "bottom-up", as it were, through the gradual improvement of animals' legal status, whereby legislative declarations of animal personhood would mean formally enshrining a position that has already been developing under the surface.[151]

Proposals for Animal Legal Status

Another question is what kind of a legal status animals *should* have. Here, scholars have made a number of proposals, which can roughly be categorised into two: those remaining within the person/thing dichotomy, and those departing from it.

First, some have advocated for the legal personhood of animals – though what they mean by "legal personhood" varies. For Wise, legal personhood means the capacity for rights, so merely declaring animals to be legal persons would not amount to much; however, the Nonhuman Rights Project has championed the fundamental right to liberty enshrined in the writ of *habeas corpus* for some animals.[152] Under the abolitionist approach, championed by Gary Francione, animals' status as property would be abolished completely, and they would receive strong fundamental rights.[153] Some other scholars writing in the common-law tradition have proposed arrangements that combine legal personhood with property status. Examples include the living property arrangement envisaged by David Favre and Angela Fernandez's

---

[149] Ownership unifies, presupposes and/or renders possible a number of other incidents of legal personhood. For instance, ownership may give rise to legal standing (i.e. the capacity to enforce the owner's property rights in court), and to at least a limited capacity to be legally harmed: if one's property rights, vested in the trust, are violated, one may be empowered to sue for compensation.

[150] Furthermore, it gives priority to animals owned by humans who have sufficient means to set up such trusts.

[151] Eva Bernet Kempers, "Transition Rather than Revolution: The Gradual Road towards Animal Legal Personhood through the Legislature" (2022) 11 Transnational Environmental Law 581.

[152] For a relatively recent account, see Steven M Wise, "The Struggle for the Legal Rights of Nonhuman Animals Begins – the Experience of the Nonhuman Rights Project in New York and Connecticut" (2019) 25 Animal Law 367.

[153] Gary Francione, *Animals, Property, and the Law* (Temple University Press 1995).

proposal for a "quasi-property" status for animals – though Fernandez's proposal can also be seen as an analysis of the current legal status of animals.[154]

Civilian jurists have also often approached the issue in terms of a new doctrinal personhood category. For instance, Stucki suggests the category of "animal persons" (*tierliche Personen*).[155] Caroline Regad and Cédric Riot have made a relatively intricate proposal. They suggest that the category of natural persons be divided into *human persons* and *non-human persons*. Furthermore, they divide the latter category into three subcategories: *companion animals*, *other domesticated animals* and *wild animals*.[156] Each subcategory would come with a distinct set of rights.[157]

A second approach involves instead at least a partial departure from the person/thing dichotomy. Tomasz Pietrzykowski, for instance, has argued that animals be granted the status of a *non-personal subject of law*, with the right to have their interests considered.[158] Maneesha Deckha, on the other hand, has argued for the third category of "legal beingness".[159]

Rights of Nature and Environmental Personhood

The Rights of Nature movement is based on a somewhat different ideology. Craig M. Kauffman and Pamela L. Martin provide a useful summary of this movement. They note first that the phrase "Rights of Nature" can be understood as (1) a legal philosophy, also known as Earth Jurisprudence, or (2) "legal provisions that codify this philosophy by recognizing ecosystems as subjects with rights".

Earth Jurisprudence is a vision of the "lawful order" of the universe:

> All elements of Nature, including humans, are inextricably connected into this order and linked to one another through interdependent relationships. Consequently, human well-being is dependent on the well-being of the ecosystems that sustain all life.[160]

---

[154] David Favre, "Living Property: A New Status for Animals within the Legal System" (2010) 93 Marquette Law Review 1021; Angela Fernandez, "Not Quite Property, Not Quite Persons: A 'Quasi' Approach for Nonhuman Animals" (2019) 5 Canadian Journal of Comparative and Contemporary Law 155.

[155] See e.g. Saskia Stucki, *Grundrechte Für Tiere. Eine Kritik Des Geltenden Tierschutzrechts Und Rechtstheoretische Grundlegund von Tierrechten Im Rahmen Einer Neupositionerung Des Tieres Als Rechtssubjekt* (Nomos 2016) 301ff.

[156] See Regad (n 142) 6. The middle category (*les animaux liés à un fonds*) includes animals used for production, entertainment and experimentation.

[157] Hence, such doctrinal personhood categories could function as "inference tickets", as discussed in Section 2.

[158] Pietrzykowski (n 39).

[159] Maneesha Deckha, *Animals as Legal Beings: Contesting Anthropocentric Legal Orders* (University of Toronto Press 2020). I should note that, under my theory of legal personhood, legal beingness might in fact ultimately be a subtype of legal personhood. Whether this is the case depends on what kind of rights (and duties) are ultimately associated with legal beingness.

[160] Kauffman and Martin (n 7) 4.

Earth Jurisprudence advocates a legal system that is modelled after this lawful order in order to address "looming climate and biodiversity crises".[161] Hence, the concern is not primarily the rights of individual (human or nonhuman) animals but rather the interdependency of all life. This vision is compatible with many indigenous worldviews, which is why the movement has many indigenous adherents as well. Rights of Nature provisions are, then, one way of attempting to integrate Earth Jurisprudence into Western legal systems. However, Kauffman and Martin note that Earth Jurisprudence and Rights of Nature provisions can also come apart. On one hand, Earth Jurisprudence could be realised without appealing to rights – in fact, the individualistic notion of rights can even be seen to be in tension with certain tenets of Earth Jurisprudence. On the other hand, nature or ecosystems could be protected by rights or legal personhood even without relying on Earth Jurisprudence. A classic example of this would likely be Christopher Stone's writings, where he advocates for rights to natural objects mostly as a practical way of improving environmental protection.[162]

One final distinction that Kauffman and Martin make is between what they call the "Nature's Rights Model" and the "Legal Personhood Model". This distinction between right-holding and legal personhood is especially pleasing, for someone whose overall theory of legal personhood distinguishes between these two concepts.

Examples of the Nature's Rights Model are Bolivia and Ecuador. Both give distinct rights to nature. For instance, Section 7 of Ecuador's constitution is devoted solely to the rights of nature. The section includes for instance Article 71(1), according to which

> Nature, or Pacha Mama, where life is reproduced and occurs, has the right to integral respect for its existence and for the maintenance and regeneration of its life cycles, structure, functions and evolutionary processes.[163]

On the other hand, the Legal Personhood Model involves giving the same kind of rights that legal persons have – including, for example, property rights – to more limited ecosystems, such as individual rivers. The potentially most famous example is the Whanganui River in New Zealand, which is treated as a legal person under the Te Awa Tupua Act.[164]

---

[161] ibid. I understand the idea of a "lawful order" to be an account of natural law, though not necessarily natural law *qua* an account of legal validity.

[162] Christopher D Stone, *Should Trees Have Standing? Law, Morality, and the Environment* (3rd ed., Oxford University Press 2010).

[163] Constitution of Ecuador, unofficial English translation.

[164] Te Awa Tupua (Whanganui River Claims Settlement) Act 2017; Public Act 2017 No 7; Date of assent 20 March 2017.

Another distinction has to do with what I have termed *direct* and *indirect* legal personhood. This distinction is inspired by the analysis of Erin O'Donnell and Elizabeth Macpherson.[165] Essentially, a legal provision may attribute legal personhood (or rights) to a natural entity directly, but a legal person may also be set up to protect a natural entity, without attributing the legal personhood to the natural object itself. Hence, for instance, mountain X could be protected by setting up a legal platform entitled "Mountain X" or "Mountain X Management Entity". Both cases might function roughly similarly in practice, even if the symbolic effects might be different.[166]

AI Legal Personhood

Lawrence Solum's 1992 article is often taken to be the prescient classic addressing the topic of legal personhood for artificial intelligence systems.[167] The idea has started receiving an increasing amount of attention in the recent years, not only from scholars but also for instance politicians. However, as is often the case with legal personhood, the topic is fraught with ambiguity. Again, we can ask similar questions as with other types of legal personhood:

(1) What would giving legal personhood to an AI system mean?
(2) Can AI systems be legal persons?
(3) Are some AI systems already legal persons?
(4) Should some AI systems be given legal personhood?

However, the section will not strictly follow this order of questions. Rather, I will first discuss question (1), but while doing so, it will be quite natural to discuss some aspects of the other questions as well.

The Meaning of AI Legal Personhood

The legal personhood of animals and nature is typically motivated by the protection of these entities. However, AI personhood may be motivated by other reasons as well. Simon Chesterman writes:

> As AI systems become more sophisticated and play a larger role in society, there are at least two discrete reasons why they might be recognised as

---

[165] Erin O'Donnell and Elizabeth Macpherson, "Voice, Power and Legitimacy: The Role of the Legal Person in River Management in New Zealand, Chile and Australia" (2019) 23 Australian Journal of Water Resources 35.

[166] Kurki, "Can Nature Hold Rights?" (n 66).

[167] Lawrence B Solum, "Legal Personhood for Artificial Intelligences" (1992) 70 North Carolina Law Review 1231. Joshua Gellers notes that Sam Lehman-Wilzig addressed these questions already in 1982. See Gellers (n 29) 35; Sam N Lehman-Wilzig, "Frankenstein Unbound: Towards a Legal Definition of Artificial Intelligence" (1981) 13 Futures 442.

persons before the law. The first is so that there is someone to blame when things go wrong. This is presented as the answer to potential accountability gaps created by their speed, autonomy, and opacity. A second reason for recognising personality, however, is to ensure that there is someone to reward when things go right. A growing body of literature examines ownership of intellectual property created by AI systems, for example.[168]

Chesterman also notes – as discussed earlier in this Element – that granting legal personhood to an AI system can be based on intrinsic or instrumental reasons. Reasons for granting legal personhood would likely be reflected in the type of ensuing legal personhood. I myself have distinguished three contexts for AI legal personhood: the *ultimate-value context, commercial context* and the *responsibility context*. These three contexts can, however, overlap to a significant extent, as will become apparent.

The ultimate-value context is quite close to what Chesterman means by "intrinsic reasons". Essentially, AI systems would be granted incidents of legal personhood for their own sake. The appropriate type of legal personhood arrangement would depend on the type of entity we are talking about. If the AI system were a robot with a bodily form, it could be granted rights protecting its physical integrity. Its autonomy and self-determination could be protected by various incidents of legal personhood, such as ownership, contracting and legal standing. The ultimate-value context is not clearly reflected in Chesterman's typology of "who to blame when things go wrong" and "who to reward when things go right". Rather, the question here is, "who or what is (morally) entitled to legal personhood". Theoretically, even purely passive legal personhood could be possible here.

What I have termed the commercial context has to do with AI systems as actors in the commercial sphere. Here, we do not merely consider robots as agents that can cause damage, but as agents that can for instance enter contracts, buy and sell stock and so on – in short, perform transactions through the use of legal competences. Another interesting question is whether an AI system could own the copyright for an artwork it has produced, or whether it could successfully file for a patent for an innovation.[169] This question can be seen as pertaining to AI ownership rights in a broad sense.[170] Again, questions such as these can be approached from an intrinsic or instrumental point of view. From an intrinsic point of view, we may think of the commercial context as being derivative of the ultimate-value context. Hence, for instance, AI systems' intellectual property

---

[168] Chesterman (n 78) 820.

[169] E.g. C Ruipérez, E Gutiérrez, C Puente, et al., "New Challenges of Copyright Authorship in AI" (The Steering Committee of The World Congress in Computer Science, 2017); W Michael Schuster, "Artificial Intelligence and Patent Ownership" (2018) 75 Washington and Lee Law Review 1945.

[170] Whether e.g. copyright or a patent right is a special type of ownership, or rather a distinct type of right, is a contested issue.

rights could be justified by reference to their (moral) right to be recognised as makers of artworks created by them.[171] However, again, the instrumental point of view is more prominent.

A relatively established way of approaching these questions – especially with regard to contracting and other transactions – has been to employ the tool/ representative/legal person trifurcation.[172] As the terms imply, treating an AI system as a tool would imply treating it like a hammer; the second category would entail applying the law of agency to, for example, transactions entered by an AI on behalf of, say, a company; and the third would involve treating the AI as a separate legal person. However, I have argued that this trifurcation in fact conflates two important aspects: (1) the extent to which the AI's legal platform – bundle of rights and duties – is treated as separate from some other legal platform (*separateness*) and (2) the extent to which the AI system is treated as a distinct actor in the eyes of the law (*independency*).[173]

Though I have earlier offered this analysis in the context of AIs as commercial actors, I now believe the question of the active legal personhood of AI systems more generally – including the responsibility context – can be approached along these lines. However, addressing this point will require first presenting the responsibility context.

The responsibility context is mainly focused on questions of responsibility when things go wrong. Given the increasing autonomy and sophistication of robots and other AI systems, traditional doctrines of how to attribute blame for harm might not be appropriate. The responsibility context may also be understood from an intrinsic or instrumental point of view. From an intrinsic point of view, we might ask whether a robot could be the kind of entity that deserves to be held responsible, or even benefits from it. For instance, treating a robot as responsible could be seen as supporting the development of the robot as a moral agent. However, the responsibility of AI systems is more often approached from an instrumentalist point of view, as performing some societal function. A central issue here has to do with the so-called responsibility gap: "the risk that no human agent might be legitimately blamed or held culpable for the unwanted

---

[171] Generally, the civil-law approach to copyright has included the idea that works created are also expressions of the author's personality. This is expressed in the doctrine of what are – for philosophers, highly confusingly – labelled "moral rights". Such rights are a subgroup of legal rights vesting in the author, including for instance the right to be recognised as the author of the work. Such rights are often inalienable, meaning that the author cannot waive them. See e.g. Emmanuel Salami, "AI-Generated Works and Copyright Law: Towards a Union of Strange Bedfellows" (2021) 16 Journal of Intellectual Property Law & Practice 124, 130–2.

[172] See e.g. Ugo Pagallo, *The Laws of Robots* (Springer 2013) 40.

[173] Kurki, *A Theory of Legal Personhood* (n 17) 132.

outcomes of actions mediated by AI systems".[174] One solution to this issue may be holding the AI system itself responsible. We can distinguish compensation and punishment here.

First consider the idea that AI systems be required to pay compensation for some of their actions. An oft-mentioned example is that of autonomous cars: if an autonomous car causes damage, could it be required to compensate for the damage itself?[175] Such an arrangement would be one solution to the responsibility gap, though many other solutions have been proposed as well, such as insurances[176] and "no-fault liability schemes", meaning statutory compensation schemes that are used to compensate for losses even when no-one is at fault.[177] Making the AI system itself liable to pay compensation would necessitate that the AI system also be able to own property and be party to transactions, and would therefore take us closer to the commercial context.

Another way of possibly filling the responsibility gap would be to punish an AI system. Some have argued that such a punishment could even serve the human psychological need for revenge.[178] An important antecedent question here is whether artificial intelligence systems even *can* be punished. For instance, Robert Sparrow has famously argued that the use of autonomous weapons systems may lead to a situation where no-one and nothing can be held responsible for, say, civilian deaths. According to Sparrow, the use such of systems leads to a genuine responsibility gap because it is impossible to punish the weapons systems themselves.[179] Many scholars, including myself, have argued that it is indeed meaningful to punish AI agents: even if they might not be meaningful objects of punishment from a retributivist point of view, other rationales of punishment, such as deterrence, may very well apply to AI agents.[180] Possible sanctions would involve economic sanctions – especially if the AI system could own property – as well as other sanctions, such as "forced labour" (using the AI system for a specific purpose), reprogramming or even destruction of the system in question.[181]

---

[174] Filippo Santoni de Sio and Giulio Mecacci, "Four Responsibility Gaps with Artificial Intelligence: Why They Matter and How to Address Them" (2021) 34 Philosophy & Technology 1057, 1059. The authors argue that there are in fact four types of responsibility gaps – the gap discussed here is what they term the "culpability gap", which they distinguish from the *moral accountability gap*, the *public accountability gap*, and the *active responsibility gap*.

[175] See e.g. Pagallo (n 173) 110.   [176] Solum (n 168) 1245.

[177] See e.g. Emiliano Marchisio, "In Support of 'No-Fault' Civil Liability Rules for Artificial Intelligence" (2021) 1 SN Social Sciences 54.

[178] Christina Mulligan, "Revenge against Robots" (2017) 69 South Carolina Law Review 579.

[179] Robert Sparrow, "Killer Robots" (2007) 24 Journal of Applied Philosophy 62.

[180] Maciek Zając, "Punishing Robots – Way Out of Sparrow's Responsibility Attribution Problem" (2020) 19 Journal of Military Ethics 285; Kurki, *A Theory of Legal Personhood* (n 17) 179–82.

[181] Samir Chopra and Laurence F White, *A Legal Theory for Autonomous Artificial Agents* (The University of Michigan Press 2011) 167–9; Chesterman (n 78) 826f.

Now, we can also distinguish the independency of responsibility from the independency of competences. This dimension tracks the question of whether harms caused by an AI system are attributed to some other party (such as its owner) or to the AI system itself. In a way, the question here is "where the buck stops". If the AI is treated as fully responsible, the buck almost always stops at the AI: harms for which it is causally responsible are, as a rule, not attributed to any other party.[182] However, there can still conceivably be similar kinds of exceptions as with the responsibility of human beings: for instance, an adult of sound mind who is in most regards fully responsible, can be misled into performing acts whose consequences they are not fully aware of. In such cases, the responsibility may ultimately lie with the party doing the misleading.

Under partial responsibility, the buck occasionally stops at the AI, but there may also be cases where some other party is held responsible for the acts of the AI. For instance, the programmers of the AI might be held responsible in some cases. Finally, under assimilation – as with the independency of competences – the AI system is essentially not treated as legally capable of performing acts at all. Like in the commercial context, whether the AI has a separate legal platform affects many issues as well. For instance, as discussed above, requiring the AI pay compensation would necessitate that the AI also controls a legal platform. These different categories are presented in Table 5.

Are Some AI Systems Already Legal Persons?

As has hopefully become clear, the question of AI legal personhood is multifaceted and multifarious. Hence – as is typical of legal personhood – the question of whether some AI systems can, are, or should be, legal persons will depend on the context.

First, can AI systems be legal persons? If one adheres to the Anything-Goes View, the answer is of course straightforward: yes, they can. If the legislator or some other appropriate legal authority decrees that some AI system is a legal person, then it is a legal person.[183] If one instead thinks that not everything can be a legal person, some account of the domain of legal personhood is required.

---

[182] This is not to say that the AI system would automatically be held responsible for harms that it has caused; the law could for instance still include a culpability requirement.

[183] For instance, David Gunkel claims that "[a]ll that is necessary for something to be recognised as a legal person [meaning "artificial person"] is for some legal authority – the head of state, a legislature, or a court of law – to decide that, for whatever reason, some specific AI has legal status as a person". Gunkel and Wales (n 67) 475. In their rather sophisticated account, Joanna Bryson, Mihailis Diamantis, and Thomas Grant describe legal personhood as a "fiction" and seem to assume that it can be attributed to more or less anything, even if they do not state this explicitly. Joanna J Bryson, Mihailis E Diamantis, and Thomas D Grant, "Of, for, and by the People: The Legal Lacuna of Synthetic Persons" (2017) 25 Artificial Intelligence and Law 273.

Table 5 Dimensions of AI legal personhood

	1	2	3
S. Separateness	1. *Unity.* AI system has no legal platform assigned to it.	2. *Partial separation.* AI-controlled legal platform partially separate and revocable	3. *Total separation.* AI-controlled legal platform completely separate and irrevocable
C. Independency of competences	1. *Assimilation.* Any exercise of competence by AI is treated as having been done by the owner/operator	2. *Dependency.* Someone can, for example, retroactively cancel contracts made by AI	3. *Independency.* Completely independent in exercise of competences
R. Independency of responsibility	1. *Assimilation.* Any "act" of the AI is treated as having been done by the owner/operator	2. *Partial responsibility.* Responsibility attributable to AI system in some cases	3. *Full responsibility.* Responsibility attributable to AI in virtually all cases.

The table tracks three dimensions on which the legal personhood of an AI can be assessed. First, separateness involves the extent to which the AI has a distinct legal platform assigned to it. The other two dimensions have to do with the two incidents of active legal personhood: competences and responsibility. The independency of competences involves whether the AI has competences of its "own", and the extent to which others may, for example, cancel or veto the AI system's exercise of competences. (On dependent and independent competences, see Section 3 on children as legal persons.) The independency of responsibility has to do with the extent to which the AI is treated as a distinct responsible subject.

I myself have argued that these limits can be determined by considering the building blocks of legal personhood: claim-rights, duties and competences, and which entities can be endowed with said building blocks.[184] However, I will not delve deeper into this question here.

A rather interesting question is whether some AI systems are *already* legal persons. There are at least two prominent potential examples. First, the robot Sophia, which was supposedly granted citizenship by Saudi Arabia.[185] However, the legal implications of this putative citizenship – if there are any – are extremely unclear. As the journalist Robert David Hart puts it,

> I presume that Sophia is not paid for the work she undertakes on behalf of Hanson Robotics, the Hong Kong-based company that created her, nor has she consented to the untold number of modifications that will have been conducted on her (both physically and "mentally"). What would we do if Sophia committed a crime, wanted to get married, or somehow applied for asylum in another country?[186]

In lack of evidence to the contrary, I take this case as nothing more than a marketing stunt.

The second, and much more interesting, example is the legal regulation of personal delivery devices, meaning small robots that deliver goods from a store to a consumer. As scholars such as David Gunkel have noted, the legislation of the state of Virginia provides that "a personal delivery device operating on a sidewalk or crosswalk shall have all the rights and responsibilities applicable to a pedestrian under the same circumstance".[187] Gunkel claims that the legislature has in fact granted rights and responsibilities to said robots. However, this interpretation may be questioned.

Gunkel's view relies on what I have termed "Rights Deference": taking legislative ascriptions of rights very literally and unquestioningly.[188] However, instead of being this deferential, one can follow Hans Kelsen's approach. Kelsen notes that a law according to which "a good which is not in time returned to the

---

[184] Kurki, *A Theory of Legal Personhood* (n 17) 138–46.

[185] A preliminary issue here is, of course, whether citizenship entails legal personhood. This conclusion is not obvious, and depends on the jurisdiction, but let us assume that this entailment holds in the case of Saudi Arabia.

[186] Robert David Hart, "Saudi Arabia's Robot Citizen Is Eroding Human Rights" (*Quartz*, 14 February 2018) https://qz.com/1205017/saudi-arabias-robot-citizen-is-eroding-human-rights/ accessed 6 October 2022.

[187] Code of Virginia, Title 46.2, subtitle III, Chapter 8, article 12, § 46.2–908.1:1.D. See David J Gunkel, "The Rights of Robots" (4 April 2022) 6–7 https://papers.ssrn.com/abstract=4077131 accessed 6 October 2022.

[188] Visa AJ Kurki, "Are Legal Positivism and the Interest Theory of Rights Compatible?" in Mark McBride and Visa AJ Kurki (eds), *Without Trimmings: The Legal, Moral, and Political Philosophy of Matthew Kramer* (Oxford University Press 2022).

sender has to be treated as if it had been approved and accepted by the receiver" need not be analysed as claiming that the receiver really has approved the goods. Instead, Kelsen takes the legislative text to be an "abbreviating expression", noting that "[i]t would be superfluous to repeat all the rules which have already been set down for the first case. The legislator can rest content with declaring that in the second case the same rules apply as in the first case".[189] Even if the Virginian legislator has not used the phrase "as if" – as in Kelsen's example – one can treat the provision as an abbreviating expression. For instance, according to the same statute, even bicycles have rights.[190] Hence, there are reasons to think that – in spite of the wording of the law – personal delivery devices and bicycles might not, in fact, be right-holders or duty-bearers. However, addressing this topic more thoroughly would require an extensive foray into theories of rights.

Regardless of whether we may plausibly reach the conclusion that personal delivery devices and bicycles hold rights and responsibilities under Virginian law, this does not yet settle the question of whether they are legal persons. Under the formal Orthodox View, all right-holders and duty-bearers are of course legal persons. However, under the Bundle Theory, the devices in question would not be legal persons, as they lack virtually all of the incidents of legal personhood. For instance, if a driver were to drive over a personal delivery vehicle, they would assumedly not be required to pay compensation to the device itself, but rather to its owner or other such party. Hence, this case is in fact a good example of the problems of the Orthodox View in explaining legal personhood.

Summing Up

This section has sought to provide an overview of three new potential categories of legal personhood: animals, nature, and AI. The emergence of these three categories – either as an object of speculation or even legal reality – pose significant challenges for the anthropocentric legal order. Whether this anthropocentrism will ultimately persist remains to be seen.

Conclusion

This Element has been intended as an overall and accessible introduction to legal personhood. It is only a slight exaggeration to say that both theoretical and

---

[189] Hans Kelsen and Cristof Kletzer (tr), "On the Theory of Juridic Fictions. With Special Consideration of Vaihinger's Philosophy of the As-If" in Maksymilian Del Mar and William Twining (eds), *Legal Fictions in Theory and Practice* (Springer 2015) 10.

[190] "Except as otherwise provided in this section, an electric power-assisted bicycle or an operator of an electric power-assisted bicycle shall be afforded all the rights and privileges, and be subject to all of the duties, of a bicycle or the operator of a bicycle. An electric power-assisted bicycle is a vehicle to the same extent as is a bicycle". Code of Virginia, Title 46.2, subtitle III, Chapter 8, article 12, § 46.2–904.1.A. I owe this point to Thomas Basbøll.

practical interest in legal personhood has exploded within the last decade or so. This development can clearly be connected to broader societal and technological changes. Challenging the anthropocentric legal order has animated the calls for animal legal personhood and Rights of Nature. The striking progress of AI is perhaps the most obvious example of how technological change can actualise new questions of legal personhood. Whereas the legal personhood of AI systems was a speculative topic for a long time, it has recently become a very real and imminent prospect.

The primary objective of this Element has not been to provide normative solutions to questions such as whether some animals should be declared legal persons. Rather, the aim has been to provide an understanding of the notion of legal personhood, required to fruitfully address these questions. As has likely become apparent, I believe these questions are usually best approached in a nuanced manner. Legal personhood is not a monolith, and not all legal persons need for instance have equal rights. This fact will become increasingly apparent if and when new types of legal persons are recognised. For instance, the rights of "animal persons" would likely be rather different from those of natural and artificial persons.

It is rather unlikely that the ongoing debate over legal personhood would die down anytime soon. Much of this debate is still often built upon unproblematised assumptions about the meaning of legal personhood. I hope that those participating in this debate will examine not only the applications but also the notion of legal personhood itself. The Orthodox View should regardless not be seen as an axiomatic truth about legal personhood, as it has occasionally been treated in the past.

Bibliography

Afrouzi AE, "Visa A. J. Kurki, A Theory of Legal Personhood, Oxford: Oxford University Press, 2019, 240 Pp, Hb £ 70.00" (2020) 83 The Modern Law Review 279

Aguilar CD, "Universal Legal Capacity to Ensure the Equal Recognition of Persons with Disabilities before the Law (Report of the Special Rapporteur on the Rights of Persons with Disabilities A/HRC/37/56)" (UN Human Rights Council 2017)

Andrews K Gary Comstock, Crozier GKD, et al., *Chimpanzee Rights: The Philosophers' Brief* (Routledge 2018)

Arstein-Kerslake A, *Legal Capacity & Gender: Realising the Human Right to Legal Personhood and Agency of Women, Disabled Women, and Gender Minorities* (Springer 2021)

"Understanding Sex: The Right to Legal Capacity to Consent to Sex" (2015) 30 Disability and Society 1459

Austin J, *Lectures on Jurisprudence: Or, the Philosophy of Positive Law, Vol. I* (John Murray, Albemarle Street 1885)

Bailey J, "Favoured or Oppressed? Married Women, Property and 'coverture' in England, 1660–1800" (2002) 17 Continuity and Change 351

Banaś P, "Why Cannot Anything Be a Legal Person?" (2021) Revus. Journal for Constitutional Theory and Philosophy of Law / Revija za ustavno teorijo in filozofijo prava.https://journals.openedition.org/revus/7335?lang=fr accessed 5 December 2022.

''Shawn Bayern, 'The Implications of Modern Business-Entity Law for the Regulation of Autonomous Systems' (2015) 19 Stanford Technology Law Review 93

Beaudry J-S, "From Autonomy to Habes Corpus: Animal Rights Activists Take the Parameters of Legal Personhood to Court" (2016) 4 Global Journal of Animal Law 3

Bryson JJ, Diamantis ME, and Grant TD, "Of, for, and by the People: The Legal Lacuna of Synthetic Persons" (2017) 25 Artificial Intelligence and Law 273

Burdick WL, *The Principles of Roman Law and Their Relation to Modern Law* (The Lawbook Exchange 2004)

Chatman CN, "If a Fetus Is a Person, It Should Get Child Support, Due Process, and Citizenship" (2020) 76 Washington and Lee Law Review Online, 91–7

Chesterman S, "Artificial Intelligence and the Limits of Legal Personality" (2020) 69 International and Comparative Law Quarterly 819

Chopra S and White LF, *A Legal Theory for Autonomous Artificial Agents* (The University of Michigan Press 2011)

Cismas I and Cammarano S, "Whose Right and Who's Right: The US Supreme Court v. the European Court of Human Rights on Corporate Exercise of Religion" (2016) 34 Boston University International Law Journal 1

Cochrane A, "Do Animals Have an Interest in Liberty?" (2009) 57 Political Studies 660

Deckha M, *Animals as Legal Beings: Contesting Anthropocentric Legal Orders* (University of Toronto Press 2020)

Dewey J, "The Historic Background of Corporate Legal Personality" (1926) 35 Yale Law Journal 655

Dhanda A, "Legal Capacity in the Disability Rights Convention: Stranglehold of the Past or Lodestar for the Future" (2007) 34 Syracuse Journal of International Law and Commerce 429

Duff PW, *Personality in Roman Private Law* (Cambridge University Press 1938)

Dyschkant A, "Legal Personhood: How We Are Getting It Wrong" (2015) University of Illinois Law Review 1231

Falguera JL, Martínez-Vidal C, and Rosen G, "Abstract Objects" in Edward N Zalta (ed), *The Stanford Encyclopedia of Philosophy* (Metaphysics Research Lab, Stanford University 2022).https://plato.stanford.edu/arch ives/sum2022/entries/abstract-objects/ accessed 19 December 2022

Fasel RN, "Shaving Ockham: A Review of Visa A. J. Kurki's 'A Theory of Legal Personhood'" (2021) 44 Revus 113–26

Favre D, "Living Property: A New Status for Animals within the Legal System" (2010) 93 Marquette Law Review 1021

Fede A, *People without Rights: An Interpretation of the Fundamentals of the Law of Slavery in the U.S. South* (Garland 1992)

Feinberg J, "The Rights of Animals and Unborn Generations" in William T Blackstone (ed), *Philosophy and Environmental Crisis* (The University of Georgia Press 1974)

Fernandez A, "Not Quite Property, Not Quite Persons: A 'Quasi' Approach for Nonhuman Animals" (2019) 5 Canadian Journal of Comparative and Contemporary Law 155

Finnis J, "The Priority of Persons" in *Intention and Identity: Collected Essays Volume II* (Oxford University Press 2011)

Foucault M, *Discipline and Punish* (Allen Lane tr, Penguin Books 1977)

Francione G, *Animals, Property, and the Law* (Temple University Press 1995)

Gaius, *Institutiones or Institutes of Roman Law* (Edward Poste tr ed., 4th ed., Clarendon Press 1904)

Gamauf R, "Slaves Doing Business: The Role of Roman Law in the Economy of a Roman Household" (2009) 16 European Review of History: Revue europeenne d'histoire 331

Gellers JC, *Rights for Robots: Artificial Intelligence, Animal and Environmental Law* (Routledge 2020)

Glackin SN, "Back to Bundles: Deflating Property Rights, Again" (2014) 20 Legal Theory 1

Gunkel DJ, "The Other Question: Can and Should Robots Have Rights?" (2017) 20 Ethics and Information Technology 1

"The Rights of Robots" (4 April 2022) https://papers.ssrn.com/abstract=4077131 accessed 6 October 2022

Gunkel DJ and Wales JJ, "Debate: What Is Personhood in the Age of AI?" (2021) 36 AI & Society 473

Harris R, "A New Understanding of the History of Limited Liability: An Invitation for Theoretical Reframing" (2020) 16 Journal of Institutional Economics 643

Hart HLA, "Definition and Theory in Jurisprudence", in *Essays in Jurisprudence and Philosophy* (Oxford University Press 1984)

The Concept of Law (Clarendon Press 1994)

Hart RD, "Saudi Arabia's Robot Citizen Is Eroding Human Rights" *Quartz*, 14 February 2018 https://qz.com/1205017/saudi-arabias-robot-citizen-is-eroding-human-rights/ accessed 6 October 2022

Hartney M, "Some Confusions Concerning Collective Rights" (1991) 4 Canadian Journal of Law & Jurisprudence 293

Hohfeld WN, "Some Fundamental Legal Conceptions as Applied in Legal Reasoning" (1913) 23 Yale Law Journal 16

Honoré AM, "Ownership" in Anthony G Guest (ed), *Oxford Essays in Jurisprudence* (Oxford University Press 1961)

Ireland P, "Limited Liability, Shareholder Rights and the Problem of Corporate Irresponsibility" (2010) 34 Cambridge Journal of Economics 837

Johnson L, "Law and Legal Theory in the History of Corporate Responsibility: Corporate Personhood Berle III: Theory of the Firm: The Third Annual Symposium of the Adolf A. Berle, Jr. Center on Corporations, Law & Society" (2011) 35 Seattle University Law Review 1135

Jowitt J, "Legal Rights for Animals: Aspiration or Logical Necessity?" (2020) 11 Journal of Human Rights and the Environment 173

Kauffman CM and Martin PL, *The Politics of Rights of Nature: Strategies for Building a More Sustainable Future* (MIT Press 2021)

Kelsen H, *General Theory of Law and State* (Transaction 2006)

Kelsen H and Kletzer (tr) C, "On the Theory of Juridic Fictions. With Special Consideration of Vaihinger's Philosophy of the As-If" in Maksymilian Del Mar and William Twining (eds), *Legal Fictions in Theory and Practice* (Springer 2015)

Kempers EB, "Transition Rather than Revolution: The Gradual Road towards Animal Legal Personhood through the Legislature" (2022) 11 Transnational Environmental Law 581

Kens P, "Nothing to Do with Personhood: Corporate Constitutional Rights and the Principle of Confiscation" (2015) 34 Quinnipiac Law Review 1

Kramer MH, "Do Animals and Dead People Have Legal Rights?" (2001) 14 Canadian Journal of Law & Jurisprudence 29

Kramer MH, "Rights without Trimmings" in Matthew H Kramer, NE Simmonds and Hillel Steiner (eds), *A Debate over Rights: Philosophical Enquiries* (Oxford University Press 1998)

Kramer MH, Simmonds NE, and Steiner H, *A Debate over Rights: Philosophical Enquiries* (Oxford University Press 1998)

Kurki V, "Active but Not Independent: The Legal Personhood of Children" (2021) 30 Griffith Law Review 395

"Expanding Agency and Borders of Competence" in Gonzalo Villa Rosas and Torben Spaak (eds), *Legal Power and Legal Competence: Meaning, Normativity, Officials and Theories* (Springer 2023)

"Rikosoikeuden Subjekti" in Esko Yli-Hemminki, Sakari Melander, and Kimmo Nuotio (eds), *Rikoksen ja rangaistuksen filosofia* (Gaudeamus 2023)

Kurki VAJ, "Animals, Slaves and Corporations: Analyzing Legal Thinghood" (2017) 18 German Law Journal 1096

"Are Legal Positivism and the Interest Theory of Rights Compatible?" in Mark McBride and Visa AJ Kurki (eds), *Without Trimmings: The Legal, Moral, and Political Philosophy of Matthew Kramer* (Oxford University Press 2022)

"Can Nature Hold Rights? It's Not as Easy as You Think" (2022) 11 Transnational Environmental Law 525

"Legal Power and Legal Competence" in Mark McBride (ed), *New Essays on the Nature of Rights* (Hart 2017)

A Theory of Legal Personhood (Oxford University Press 2019)

Lavonius W, *Vuosikertomus Eläintensuojelus-Yhdistyksen Helsingissä yleiseen kokoukseen* (Eläintensuojelus-Yhdistys Helsingissä 1876)

Lawson FH, "The Creative Use of Legal Concepts" (1957) 32 New York University Law Review 909

Lehman-Wilzig SN, "Frankenstein Unbound: Towards a Legal Definition of Artificial Intelligence" (1981) 13 Futures 442

Lindroos-Hovinheimo S, *Private Selves: Legal Personhood in European Privacy Protection* (Cambridge University Press 2021)

List C and Pettit P, *Group Agency: The Possibility, Design, and Status of Corporate Agents* (Oxford University Press 2011)

MacCormick N, *Institutions of Law: An Essay in Legal Theory* (Oxford University Press 2007)

"Persons as Institutional Facts" in Ota Weinberger and Werner Krawietz (eds), *Reine Rechtslehre im Spiegel ihrer Fortsetzer und Kritiker* (Springer 1988)

Mäntysaari P, *Organising the Firm: Theories of Commercial Law, Corporate Governance and Corporate Law* (Springer-Verlag 2012)

Marchisio E, "In Support of 'No-Fault' Civil Liability Rules for Artificial Intelligence" (2021) 1 SN Social Sciences 54

May T, "Subjectification" in Leonard Lawlor and John Nale (eds), *The Cambridge Foucault Lexicon* (1st ed., Cambridge University Press 2014) 496

McCausland C, "The Five Freedoms of Animal Welfare Are Rights" (2014) 27 Journal of Agricultural and Environmental Ethics 649–62

Millon D, "Theories of the Corporation" (1990) 1990 Duke Law Journal 201

Moore MS, *Placing Blame: A Theory of the Criminal Law* (Oxford University Press 2010)

Morris TD, *Southern Slavery and the Law, 1619–1860* (The University of North Carolina Press 1996)

Mulligan C, "Revenge against Robots" (2017) 69 South Carolina Law Review 579

Naffine N, *Law's Meaning of Life: Philosophy, Religion, Darwin and the Legal Person* (Hart 2009)

"Legal Personality and the Natural World: On the Persistence of the Human Measure of Value" (2012) 3 Journal of Human Rights and the Environment 68

Nilsson A, "Who Gets to Decide? Right to Legal Capacity for Persons with Intellectual and Psychosocial Disabilities" (Council of Europe Commissioner for Human Rights 2012). https://wcd.coe.int/ViewDoc.jsp?p=&id=1908555&direct=true

Novelli C, Bongiovanni G, and Sartor G, "A Conceptual Framework for Legal Personality and Its Application to AI" (2022) 13 Jurisprudence 194

O'Donnell E and Macpherson E, "Voice, Power and Legitimacy: The Role of the Legal Person in River Management in New Zealand, Chile and Australia" (2019) 23 Australian Journal of Water Resources 35

O'Donnell EL and Talbot-Jones J, "Creating Legal Rights for Rivers: Lessons from Australia, New Zealand, and India" (2018) 23 Ecology and Society 7

Orts EW, *Business Persons: A Legal Theory of the Firm* (Oxford University Press 2013)

Pagallo U, *The Laws of Robots* (Springer 2013)

Pietrzykowski T, "The Idea of Non-Personal Subjects of Law" in Visa AJ Kurki and Tomasz Pietrzykowski (eds), *Legal Personhood: Animals, Artificial Intelligence and the Unborn* (Springer 2017)

Raz J, "On the Nature of Rights" (1984) 93 XCIII Mind 194

Regad C, "Les animaux liés à un fonds, vers une nouvelle categorie de personnes physiques non-humaines" in Caroline Regad and Cédric Riot (eds), *La personnalité juridique de l'animal (II): Les animaux liés à un fonds (les animaux de rente, de divertissement, d'expérimentation)* (LexisNexis 2020)

Regan T, *The Case for Animal Rights* (University of California Press 2004)

Ross A, *On Law and Justice* (Jakob vH Holtermann ed., Uta Binreiter tr, Oxford University Press 2019)

Ruipérez C, E Gutiérrez, C Puente, et al., "New Challenges of Copyright Authorship in AI" (The Steering Committee of The World Congress in Computer Science, 2017)

Sachs B, *Contractarianism, Role Obligations, and Political Morality* (Routledge 2022)

Salami E, "AI-Generated Works and Copyright Law: Towards a Union of Strange Bedfellows" (2021) 16 Journal of Intellectual Property Law & Practice 124

Santoni de Sio F and Mecacci G, "Four Responsibility Gaps with Artificial Intelligence: Why They Matter and How to Address Them" (2021) 34 Philosophy & Technology 1057

Saunders HD, "Civil Death: A New Look at an Ancient Doctrine" (1970) 11 William and Mary Law Review 988

Schuster WM, "Artificial Intelligence and Patent Ownership" (2018) 75 Washington and Lee Law Review 1945

Searle J, *Making the Social World: The Structure of Human Civilization* (Oxford University Press 2010)

Seymour J, *Childbirth and the Law* (Oxford University Press 2000)

Siltala R, "Earth, Wind, and Fire, and Other Dilemmas in a Theory of Legal Personhood – a Vindication of Legal Conventionalism" (2021) Revus. Journal for Constitutional Theory and Philosophy of Law / Revija za ustavno teorijo in filozofijo prava 137–46 https://journals.openedition.org/revus/6974 accessed 20 November 2022

Solaiman SM, "Legal Personality of Robots, Corporations, Idols and Chimpanzees: A Quest for Legitimacy" (2017) 25 Artificial Intelligence and Law 155

Solum LB, "Legal Personhood for Artificial Intelligences" (1992) 70 North Carolina Law Review 1231

Sparrow R, "Killer Robots" (2007) 24 Journal of Applied Philosophy 62

Steinbock B, *Life before Birth: The Moral and Legal Status of Embryos and Fetuses* (2nd ed., Oxford University Press 2011)

Stone CD, *Should Trees Have Standing? Law, Morality, and the Environment* (3rd ed., Oxford University Press 2010)

Stucki S, *Grundrechte Für Tiere: Eine Kritik Des Geltenden Tierschutzrechts Und Rechtstheoretische Grundlegund von Tierrechten Im Rahmen Einer Neupositionerung Des Tieres Als Rechtssubjekt* (Nomos 2016)

"Towards a Theory of Legal Animal Rights: Simple and Fundamental Rights" (2020) 40 Oxford Journal of Legal Studies 533

Sunstein C, "Can Animals Sue?" in Cass R Sunstein and Martha C Nussbaum (eds), *Animal Rights: Current Debates and New Directions* (Oxford University Press 2004)

Tuori K, *Properties of Law: Modern Law and after* (Cambridge University Press 2021)

Tur R, "The 'Person' in Law" in Arthur Peacocke and Grant Gillett (eds), *Persons and Personality. A Contemporary Inquiry* (Basil Blackwell 1988)

Vaihinger H, *The Philosophy of "As If": A System of the Theoretical, Practical and Religious Fictions of Mankind* (2nd ed., Kegan Paul, Trench, Trubner 2006)

von Savigny FC, *System des heutigen römischen Rechts* (Veit 1840)

Wapler F, "Kinderrechte" in Johannes Drerup (ed), *Handbuch Philosophie der Kindheit* (J B Metzler Verlag 2019)

Warren MA, *Moral Status: Obligations to Persons and Other Living Things* (Oxford University Press 1997)

Watson A, *Roman Slave Law* (The Johns Hopkins University Press 1988)

"Roundtable: When Does Life Legally Begin? Legislative and Judicial Power in America's Abortion Debate" Washington and Lee Law Review Online https://lawreview.wlulaw.wlu.edu/category/online/roundtables/fetal-personhood/ accessed 19 December 2022

Wise SM, "A New York Appellate Court Takes a First Swing at Chimpanzee Personhood and Misses" (2017) 95 Denver Law Review 265

Rattling the Cage: Toward Legal Rights for Animals (Perseus 2000)

"The Struggle for the Legal Rights of Nonhuman Animals Begins – the Experience of the Nonhuman Rights Project in New York and Connecticut" (2019) 25 Animal Law 367

Zając M, "Punishing Robots – Way Out of Sparrow's Responsibility Attribution Problem" (2020) 19 Journal of Military Ethics 285

Acknowledgements

I am very thankful to the Series Editors for the invitation to write this Element. Over the course of the writing process, very good comments on the manuscript were provided by at least Kelly Dhru, Veerle Platvoet, Marina Baptista Rosa, and Iris Pitkänen – and probably some people I am forgetting here. The two referees provided very helpful and friendly feedback. I thank the Law Faculty of the University of Helsinki for supporting the open access publication of this booklet.

For most other good things, I thank Line.

Cambridge Elements

Philosophy of Law

Series Editors

George Pavlakos

University of Glasgow

George Pavlakos is Professor of Law and Philosophy at the School of Law, University of Glasgow. He has held visiting posts at the universities of Kiel and Luzern, the European University Institute, the UCLA Law School, the Cornell Law School and the Beihang Law School in Beijing. He is the author of *Our Knowledge of the Law* (2007) and more recently has co-edited *Agency, Negligence and Responsibility* (2021) and *Reasons and Intentions in Law and Practical Agency* (2015).

Gerald J. Postema

University of North Carolina at Chapel Hill

Gerald J. Postema is Professor Emeritus of Philosophy at the University of North Carolina at Chapel Hill. Among his publications count *Utility, Publicity, and Law: Bentham's Moral and Legal Philosophy* (2019); *On the Law of Nature, Reason, and the Common Law: Selected Jurisprudential Writings of Sir Matthew Hale* (2017); *Legal Philosophy in the Twentieth Century: The Common Law World* (2011), *Bentham and the Common Law Tradition*, 2nd edition (2019).

Kenneth M. Ehrenberg

University of Surrey

Kenneth M. Ehrenberg is Professor of Jurisprudence and Philosophy at the University of Surrey School of Law and Co-Director of the Surrey Centre for Law and Philosophy. He is the author of *The Functions of Law* (2016) and numerous articles on the nature of law, jurisprudential methodology, the relation of law to morality, practical authority, and the epistemology of evidence law.

Associate Editor

Sally Zhu

University of Sheffield

Sally Zhu is a Lecturer in Property Law at University of Sheffield. Her research is on property and private law aspects of platform and digital economies.

About the Series

This series provides an accessible overview of the philosophy of law, drawing on its varied intellectual traditions in order to showcase the interdisciplinary dimensions of jurisprudential enquiry, review the state of the art in the field, and suggest fresh research agendas for the future. Focussing on issues rather than traditions or authors, each contribution seeks to deepen our understanding of the foundations of the law, ultimately with a view to offering practical insights into some of the major challenges of our age.

Cambridge Elements$^{\equiv}$

Philosophy of Law

Elements in the Series

Printed in the United States
by Baker & Taylor Publisher Services